TOGETHER WE CRIED

a warrior's heart…a nation's son…a mother's hope

By Granda Lea Chambers

"constant prayer was offered to God for him by the church."

Acts 12:5

Shepherds
Publishing

ISBN: 978-1-09722-068-7

Shepherds Publishing, 515 6th St., P.O. Box 267 Covington, IN 47932 • 765-793-2177
shepherdspublishing.com
shepherdspublishing@yahoo.com
Shepherds Publishing on Facebook

Book layout/design by: Word Services Unlimited
loralee@wordservicesunlimited.com
wordservicesunlimited.com

Cover layout/design by: Sunny Wilderman

Printed in the United States of America.

On the front cover is Lance Corporal Bryan Chambers.
On the back cover is Sergeant Chad M. Allen, who was killed in the IED blast which devastated Bryan.

TABLE OF CONTENTS

FOREWORD

In late summer of 2018, we had the privilege of reconnecting with my best friend from my high school days, Andy Harkleroad, after almost 30 years. My dear friend was the Pastor of an awesome congregation of Christ loving believers and I had the joy of watching him minister and love on a beautiful assembly of believers. There was a concurrent joy in seeing their love and support for their Pastor and my brother in Christ. During that special weekend with Pastor Andy and his wife Pam, I had the privilege of giving the morning message from the pulpit of Andy's church and it was after the service, that we had the incredible privilege of meeting Craig and Granda Chambers.

As they related the story of their son, Bryan, and their journey of faith with him through the trauma of devastating injuries received while serving in this great nation's military, a well-known adage among those in armed forces community rang with clarity in my soul — ***"in the military, the whole family serves"***. The men and women — who stand as the thin line between evil and innocence, between oppressors and the oppressed, between bondage and freedom — can only carry out their perilous but vital mission with the support of mothers, fathers, spouses and children who lend to this nation their sons, daughters, husbands, wives, mothers and fathers for the defense of our country and our values around the world.

Craig and Granda are the paradigm of this truth. They served this nation by giving to our great republic, their son, Bryan, for the defense of liberty. Their heroic service did not end with Bryan's tragic injuries, peril wrought road of physical recovery and the ongoing trial of psychological and emotional healing. As the whole family serves with their military member, so the entire family is scarred when their warrior is wounded; on the battlefield of recovery, all still serve! With Bryan's injuries, both physical and mental, Craig and Granda entered a battlefield that very few can comprehend. It was a battlefield that they did not enter alone. As I listened to their story and you will read in pages of this account, they continuously placed their trust in the mighty hand of their loving Lord, Jesus Christ. Their faith was a tried faith; tested, with times of doubt, times of desperation, confusion, loneliness and temptation to embrace hopelessness. In reading these pages, one will encounter, in the life and story of Granda, Craig and Bryan, the true meaning of valor in the most epic sense.

KEVIN G. BROWNE, Chaplain, Maj, USAF (Ret)
M.Div, M.A.C.I., M.A.

Chapter 1
BEGINNINGS

I was *suddenly* very afraid.

Had I just made the *biggest* mistake of my life?

How could I have allowed Kim to persuade me to come to this college in the first place? Had I lost all sound judgment when I believed I could enroll in college with next to *no* money down? I had just given the gracious lady at the admissions office all the money I had. It was not nearly enough. She reluctantly gave me my meal ticket for the upcoming month. I had an additional four weeks to find a job and pay the semester in full. *What* was I thinking? My friends had dispersed with errands of their own and we were to meet back at the old post office building. I waited casually as if I hadn't a care in the world.

The three of us had made the journey from Sioux City, Iowa to Chattanooga, Tennessee. We had arrived the night before in my 1967 Chrysler New Yorker. It had plenty of room and a cavernous trunk, but I hadn't needed the space. Dreams don't take up much room.

As the crowd parted, my eyes rested upon the familiar face of my childhood friend Kim. He was not alone as he zig-zagged his way toward our meeting place. With great excitement, Kim introduced me to his close friend Craig. Within minutes I understood why Kim liked him so much.

During the course of that distressing first semester, I found a job that allowed me to stay in college and my friendship with Craig grew. The question of whether I had made a mistake in coming to Tennessee Temple was settled. No, it was not a mistake. I was exactly were God wanted me to be. I had met my future husband and I knew it. Craig was very out -going, had great wit, and he was fearless. He was exactly my opposite.

Although he was known to be relentless and bold in the pursuit of a lovely face, by Christmas of that year, I was his sole pursuit. We were married in the fading summer days of 1978 after we had finished an exciting yet exhausting summer at a children's camp.

The blending of our two lives into one began a cautious journey of transparency about our families and their differences. His family fascinated me. Theirs was a postcard picture of a traditional all-American family complete with a loving father figure. They even had a dog named King. My home could not have been more different. Not only did we have a missing father in our home, we experienced a harsh hand-to-mouth existence with dark secrets. And I didn't even have a dog. What happened in those hopeless years without the protective presence of a father splintered our sibling relationships and sent all of us running from our childhood.

Those gut-wrenching years had a profound influence on who I was and on the mother I would become. I longed to have a stable family where a child would be safe and valued for the treasured gift he or she was. With a husband like Craig, my life felt secure and our love for God and each other grew strong.

As our jam-packed first year progressed, we were dumbfounded to find ourselves pregnant. How could *that* have happened? Sorrowfully the pregnancy ended in a painful miscarriage. My second pregnancy was heaven-sent. She was a healthy, blonde haired, blue-eyed beauty. She embodied the definition of her name in the baby book of names whose pages I had worn thin from searching. Jennifer was our "white wave" who stirred up continuous ripples from the moment we brought her home from the hospital in East Ridge Tennessee. Once more with great distress, I lost our third child. Our fourth baby arrived after Craig graduated from college and we had moved back to his hometown in rural Indiana. Hollie Mae was our Christmas in July baby, a true gift from God. She was born prematurely, but she was a peaceful brown-eyed beauty. We were in love. Again.

Ongoing health issues meant I might not be able to have the little boy we so desired to complete our family. The written account of Hannah in the Old Testament intrigued me, and I followed her example. I prayed for this much desired little boy. With great hopefulness I named and willingly dedicated Bryan to the Lord before I became pregnant. His name meant brave, virtuous, strong, and honorable. These were characteristics I longed to have in a son.

The months leading up to Bryan's birth were not without unwelcome complications which foreshadowed his birth. When the long-awaited day came to deliver our son, he was born premature and lifeless. My audible cry for Bryan's life was immediate and intense. In those suspended moments of time, with hot tears of anguish, I cried out for this infant son of mine. My plea was that I would be allowed to raise this child for whom I had prayed so intently.

It had long ago been settled that he belonged to God, but my hope was to experience life as his mother. I pleaded for him to live! The answer came with a startling vision of a future event in his life. In a nanosecond I saw a young man holding a rifle dressed in military fatigues. Oddly he was standing in a sea of sand. Immediately I knew I was seeing a glimpse into his future. It was as if the Spirit of the living God was granting me a choice.

Now! Quickly! I could yield up his life and not live through the future vision or I could experience the love and joy of this child for numbered days. I chose life. I clung to life. His life.

As time hung suspended, the doctors, nurses and technicians worked feverishly over his pasty, lifeless form. The ensuing minutes and seconds brought the blessed sounds of a newborn's cry. As I cradled this heartfelt blessing of mine, kissed his little toes, marveled at his tiny perfect features, I held sealed in my bewildered mother's heart the vision of a later day.

Delighted to have the chance my mother never had, Craig and I agreed that I could be a stay at home mother. With wondered thankfulness I took great pleasure in growing up alongside these precious gifts from God my Father. I thoroughly enjoyed the days of their childhood which sprouted roots that grew deep in the soil of devoted family love and adventure. We shared our active belief in the Lord Jesus Christ with our children. Ours was a happy home.

The years grew wings and flew by in breathless intensity. Each of our children were prepared to make their own way. With bittersweet tears of joy and sorrow, I watched my daughters leave home one by one. Each time, I prayed that God would make their paths straight and bind their hearts to His. I released them to the care of a sovereign God who knew them personally, loved them deeply and had a plan for their future. As I adjusted to a household without my daughters it proved harder than I had imagined. In a blink of an eye, it was just Craig, me and Bryan.

In the summer of 2004, between our son's junior and senior years of high school, Bryan announced his decision to join the United States Marine Corps. He appealed for our approval. We were at the same time both proud and terrified. It would appear we had been very naive at gathering the many clues he had left strewn along the path of his childhood. Memories quickly reminded us that he had spent much of his childhood in the woods stealthily hiding behind trees always with a handmade weapon in his possession. We now remembered how he stayed glued to the television as the Twin Towers came down. We remembered the look on his face. As my mind replayed the memories, my heart knew I was looking at a future United States Marine.

There had been a tight-fisted handful of times in his young life when I had pried open my closed heart to the events of his birth. Now with trembling emotions I would examine the memories that bewildered me.

Uneasily I would consider whether the vision I saw could possibly come to pass. Hadn't I just imagined it? Each time after heartfelt probing, I would reassure myself that our nation was not at war. Except now we were! We had been a nation at war on terror since that dreadful day in September of 2001.

My own personal war of terror gripped my heart and imagination as the vision at his birth took on a life of its own and played over and over on the IMAX theater screen of my mind. I had not shared my abrupt glimpse into Bryan's future with anyone. Ever. I wouldn't even talk to God about it. I had persuaded myself that to speak of it was to breathe life into the vision and make it real. I comforted myself with self-talk. I had been overly distraught by the trauma of his birth. I couldn't possibly have seen what I thought I saw?! Ridiculous! Even to share such things with my husband would qualify me as a loon. Startled in those frozen moments, I realized that perhaps I had not been such a loon after all. I trembled. Was the time for its fulfillment beginning?

It was painful to consider that his young life could be nearing the final chapters. Slowly I released the vision from my sealed heart. I reluctantly opened it to repeated examinations with many tears of hot protest to my God. As I wrestled with God's decree for Bryan's future, I cried out in prayer for direction. What should I do with the foresight that I had been given? I had withheld it from my husband and my son. I knew that if I told Bryan, I might be able to convince him not to join the military, but would I dare attempt to stop the decree of God in my son's life by manipulating him?

Bryan decided to join the Marine Corps on a delayed entry program. He would finish his senior year of high school and leave for boot camp following graduation. All too quickly his senior year was behind us. Sunday dawned bright on that clear June morning. The Marine recruiter would soon be there to pick Bryan up.

I remember the events through a haze of emotion complete with still shots forever frozen in my mind's eye. Our family gathered in the living room sharing intimate talk and re-experiencing memories. We were trying to be strong for each other. After a brief introduction to his recruiter, we said our goodbyes and watched as our son walked out of our home. He wore green khakis, a pair of sneakers and a simple t-shirt. He carried nothing but a part of our hearts intertwined in his.

Left: Baby Bryan pictured with his siblings, Jennifer and Hollie.
Right: Bryan pictured right before entering book camp.

Chapter 2
THE RECRUIT

The first few weeks of boot camp crawled by in silence. Soon mail from "This Recruit" began to arrive. We were overjoyed to hear from him. His letters were always very informative, and his personality leapt off the pages. Bryan always gave us something to smile about.

Hey family,

I am writing in the dark so bear with me. Well today is July 7 and tomorrow is T1, the first day of training. All the days before this have been forming. It's been crazy since they got us on the bus. We got at MCRD (Marine Corps Recruit Depot) at night and the fun began. It has been non-stop yelling since I got…oops…not "I" but "this recruit." That has been tough to do so I just stay quiet and we are told to yell. I have signed so many papers so many times and I have a new signature. Kinda reminds me of Dads because it has an E in it. Ok my address is as follows:

Recruit Chambers, Bryan, E.
3RD, M CO, PLT 3106
39001 Midway Ave.
San Diego CA

That's a long address and it will take a while to get any mail from you guys but that's ok. I get more sleep here then I did at home. Go to bed around 2200 and wake up at 0600. I am in Mike Company "Mighty Mike!" we yell that a lot. I have almost lost my voice from all the yelling we do. The DIs are always yelling at us, but you get used to it after a while. I am slowly getting used to it. Well I am fine and holding up pretty good not messing up as bad as the other recruits. I can now eat breakfast in under 3 mins but that is a lot of food, not the best, but a lot of it. Even when we eat, we have DIs yelling at us. Don't send anything but letters and prayers. Sunday was pretty cool — like 1,200 Marines/ Recruits all worshiping was cool. I love you all. I will wright more later. I know I spelled right wrong. Again, I love you all. Bryan E Chambers

The family letter we received from our son lifted our spirits. We laughed over his spelling. Wright, right, ur…write?? The information gleaned gave vision to my imagination. I now had an entire company of 1,200 worshiping recruits to tuck secure inside my mother's heart and pray for.

On July 10 we received another letter.

Hey family,

Well this is the first real Sunday here and we get free time to write and go to church. Right now, I am waiting to go to church.

This week has been all right. I am getting used to boot camp. This platoon is slowly getting used to sounding off and doing stuff right and fast. We still get yelled at but that will never change. A third phase recruit, that is right before you graduate, said the stress in boot camp stays the same — what changes is who applies it. It shifts from the Drill Instructors applying it to the recruits applying it. Hey please pray for my safety and health. Everyone gets a cough at boot camp but pray it's only a cough. If you get sick or broken, they drop you to another company which sets back your graduation time and you might have to do training days over. I have blisters on my hands from MCMAP (Marine Corp Martial Arts Program) from hitting the bag over and over. Yesterday our squad bay got tore apart. That means 38 bunks got turned upside down, 76 racks (beds). Messed up our boots and shoes thrown everywhere. All because we didn't sound off loud enough. We had one hour to clean it all up. They also put liquid laundry detergent everywhere. It was a big mess, but we cleaned it up and now it looks the exact same as it did before. I have a positive outlook though and as Hollie said "It's just one foot in front of the other or as we say, chow to chow." You can make it to breakfast after that you can make it to lunch and then to dinner and then all over again. The rest of the week has been drill, drill, drill but it's alright. It's better than standing around getting yelled at. We have done class on

Marine Corps History, first aid and MCUJ and some other classes. Could you please send some stamps and a copy of that training matrix that tells us what we are going to do. Don't send stamps right away I have enough to last a while. Well I love and miss all of you and right now I would love to be working with dad lol (laugh out loud)!! Write to you next week. Love Bryan.

I gleaned many things from his letter. One thing in particular stood out. He was certainly being challenged mentally by all the yelling. I would pray not only for his body but especially for his mind. The highlight of our week was when our mailman delivered a letter from Bryan. I was often working in my flower garden as I waited for the coveted letters to arrive. I had a gorgeous garden that year!

July 17

Hey family,

Well it is Sunday before I go to church. It seems this is the only time I get to write to you guys. :(I got your letters and they were a big encouragement.

Wow what a busy week it has been! That is pugil sticks. (He drew a simple pencil sketch). It is for training for when you run out of bullets. The top part is the knife and the bottom is the buttstock of the rifle.

It sounds like it was a really busy week for you all with the kids and everything. I wish I could have been there. Two weeks left down here till we go up north to Pendleton for 2nd phase. This week has been a lot of drilling. That means marching movements with weapons.

We have also learned how to clean the rifle and how to put it all back together. This Saturday is Initial drill. Which is a big competition on base against all the other platoons in Mike company. We also did the obstacle course. Again, the rope is giving me a hard time. The rope is about 40 feet in the air, and we are supposed to climb up using our legs and feet. Well I got about 35 feet up and my legs start to slip so I am holding myself up with my arms. Fully rested, I could hold myself up for a while but the amount we have been using our arms it gets pretty hairy. I have always made it up but still. It is the only thing that gives me trouble on the O course.

Over a ton Dad! That by far is the biggest load ever, should have helped you before I left. Sounds like a lot of great movies coming out soon. Wish I could see them with you guys. Hollie will have to tell me how they are. Well physically I thought boot camp was going to be harder, not that it's easy by any means, it is hard as a rock, but I thought it would be tougher. Mentally on the other hand was way worse than I thought. No matter what we do, how fast we do it, or how loud we are it is never enough. It will be 2nd phase before I can write on the time we get at night. Most of the time we get to trash our house because of something then we spend the time cleaning it up.

Well I went to Medical Friday for a very small ankle sprain. I wouldn't have gone but they were having a very hard Strength and Endurance run. The SDI said to go to medical, so I went. Started to get shin splints. They hurt more when I run. Right now, I could probably get 6 pull-ups. We are all just so wore out. Time is going by pretty fast — almost a month. I just keep going from chow to chow. I have made some friends here. Basically, my bunkmate Bishop and the guys around my bunk but never really any time to talk to each other. We have had about 4 people dropped to a lower company because of sickness and other reasons. There is a Company that graduates every 2 weeks so that if you fail something like practice 9, which is a long way away, but it's a test of 160 questions. 10 practical stations where we have to do stuff like put on bandages and first aid stuff), but if we failed it, we would pick up with another company.

2nd phase goes by really quick. They say the first week is learning to shoot the rifle. Second is shooting the rifle and then the Crucible week. Hopefully it goes by quick. Well that's been my week. Pretty full of a lot of drill and getting smoked. That's where we get I'Ted...going from push-ups to jumping jacks to push-ups to crunches as fast as the DI says so we are constantly moving, when you are done — or I should say when the DI is done with you, you are dripping sweat. We drink a lot of water. A water bowl is about 40 oz and we drink 8-10 a day. One every night before we go to bed. So, you have to get up and go at night. They say if your pee is clear you aren't drinking enough water.

OH let's see! My Kodak moment so far is when we drill on the parade deck. That is where we will be graduating at. NO cars are allowed on it. It has been around for years and Marines from WW1 have walked on the deck.

Not too many Highlights. Some good stories but they need to be told in person which I will do when I get home.

I love you all and will write again as soon as I can. Love Bryan.

No one told a story quite like our son. We would not forget to prompt him to tell them when he got home.

The next weekly update was written on July 24, 2005.

Hey family,

It's Sunday again. I am sitting in the squad bay after getting the "missions" done. Missions are jobs the DIs give us to do after they put us on square-away time. It has been a long week. I don't really remember what we did though — so much.. Just nothing really remembered. If you could send me a copy of the training matrix I could recap each day. I don't think I'll be able to write next Sunday because we are moving up North. Well Initial drill was yesterday. We almost won. We lost by 3 points. That is really, really close. We had drilled so much and worked so hard to win but there was a couple people in the platoon that made a mistake, but we lost as a team. Right after Initial drill we had a mock Physical Fitness Test. It is a test Marines do every 6 months. It was just a test though, we will have the real one this Friday before we go up North. I passed the mock one with 7 pull ups 99 crunches in 2 minutes and a 3-mile run in 23:40. Not the best, definitely, not the worst. The minimums are 3 pull-ups, 50 crunches, and a 28:00 run time. I am about average.

Man, I miss you guys so much. It is so much more real now. I almost got to call you yesterday. The whole platoon almost got a phone call. That would have happened if we had won Initial Drill. So, the whole platoon was mad we lost. Before we found out we got 2nd they told us we got 6th and then "smoked" us all. That is when we get PT a lot. I think I told you guys about it. Then we got our house tore apart worse than ever. Our footlockers were dropped in a big pile and our C bags. We took all our mattresses off the racks and put them in the middle of the squad bay. Let's just say it was a BIG mess. But we got it cleaned up in time for lights out and taps. Taps is by far the best part of the day. It is the start of 7-8 hours of not getting messed with by the DIs. Hey Hollie, how's that Harry Potter book? Read about it in the paper. Sounds pretty sweet. Well I've almost made it through phase 1 without getting hurt or dropped. What an answer to prayer that is! I don't want to be here longer than I have to. Now just to get through phase 2 and 3. They say phase 2 is were getting hurt is more likely because of all the hiking and field stuff.

I have managed to save all your letters even when our house is getting torn apart. Other than the training matrix just send letters. They are so much of a booster.

Well I got to do some more stuff before our time ends. I love you all and wish I could be there.

Love you all so, so much, Bryan "Recruit Chambers"

As I read his letters, I received insight into my son's mind and sentimental heart. Insight into the Marine Corps too. I had much to pray about. For the third time I enclosed a copy of the Training Matrix he had asked for. It occurred to me that whoever was going through the mail was discarding the training matrix.

July 31, 2005

Hey family,

WOW what a week! Monday, I went to Dental. I didn't know I had dental, but I went and got two fillings. They numbed my mouth. After that we had Swim 1 which was ok. We had to swim across a pool with our camis on. Not hard at all… then we had to jump off the diving board and stay afloat for 5 mins. Tuesday, we did chokes and counter to chokes. The martial arts the Marine Corps teaches is really, really basic not as fun as I thought it would be. Wednesday, we did the CCX course — not sure what CCX stands for but it was a bayonet assault course. It was fun. Hey, I just asked the date and it is the 31st. And THAT day is special. Happy Birthday Hollie wish I could be there. I have to take you out for a late birthday party when I get back. OK. Well Wednesday we did pugil sticks 3 — that is the final battle. We run into a room and fight it out. I won my fight. I almost knocked out the other guy. It was a pretty hard hit. the DIs had to pull me off him. It was fun. Friday, we had a Series Inspection. It was very boring — stood at attention for like 4 hours. It was a long day.

Saturday was a black day. Kinda like black Friday but worse. It was move day to up North. Our C bags weighed about 70 pounds and we were running around the base around trees and back and over and over. Then we dumped them all over the squad bay and had to set up the house. All our stuff got mixed up but that's okay. We are all so used to that so not a big deal. Next week they say is really going to be boring. Nothing but dry firing the M16 learning how to shoot and the different positions.

Well enough about me. Thanks for all your letters. They are such an encouragement. The pics are really nice. Great to hear everything is going good. Sounds like it's busy but that is a good thing. That Harry Potter sounds great Hollie. Hey is that death 1 of the 3 or someone else? Well I got to wrap it up church is in 15 mins. I love you all and hope and pray you have a good week.

Love "Chambers" Bryan

Receiving his letters was as if we were taking an audited course of Marine Corps boot camp training. Bryan did an excellent job informing us. We were faithfully praying and crossing off the calendar days till we would see Bryan again. Thankfully his letters kept coming.

August 7

Hey family,

Well it's an interesting week to recap but before I do that let me answer a few questions from your letters.

Church is pretty cool when I get to go. I don't go every Sunday because we have a lot to get done. So much stuff has to be done on Sunday mornings. Ok Dad and as for the food

... Well, all the guys get excited when we get to eat MREs. Remember that thing I ate after coming home from

Denver? Well those are better than the Government chow food. The chow isn't that bad but not a lot and weird combinations.

Next question. A platoon size varies but 3106 started with 81 recruits and as of right now 3106 is at 71 and they say before we graduate it will be down in the 60's. Ok back to more questions. I got a Bible at the PX which is the base store. I had to buy it, but it was like 7 bucks so no big deal. I got it like 3 weeks after I got here. I try to read it often. I sometimes get up at night and go to the head and read it there. Thank you for all your prayers they have been working. Just keep praying especially for my feet they have some smaller blisters on them. OK now for the week recap. Well, it was snap in. We all get in big circles and dry fire the weapons. Tuesday, we had a 3-mile hike with our packs. That was no problem at all real cake walk. From Tuesday to Saturday just more snapping in. Saturday, we had a 5- mile hike which was harder because we had flak jackets on and our Kevlar helmets. The flak jackets raise your core body temp by 8 degrees so that puts your core body temp at 100 degrees or so then your helmet adds 1 or 2 degrees to the mix, so you are hiking 5 miles almost overheating the whole way there. 2 guys from our platoon fell out of the hike which means they didn't make it. They might get dropped. 3 weeks left up North. Next week is firing week.

We spend most of the week shooting and working in the pit. The pit is where the targets are. We put shot spotters on the target and send it back up so the people that are shooting can see where they hit. The Marines shot at targets at 500 yards. That's a big thing for open sights.

Let's put it this way. The Army snipers to pass sniper school have to shoot at 500 yards that means every Marine is better than an Army sniper because we do it with open sights not with a scope. MARINES ROCK! The last two weeks of training up North are the hardest. After that smooth because 3rd phase is graduation prep nothing really physical. Just our final test...final drill so, really, I have only 3 weeks left of real boot camp.

Hey, make sure you put me on your travel plans so we can be on the same flight home. I'll pay you for the ticket. Not sure how much money I will have after boot camp.

There is more expenses than I thought there would be after the uniforms and stuff. I'll probably have go to SOI (School of Infantry) with like 400 bucks but that is fine by me. I also might get a tattoo. I haven't decided yet but been thinking about it. Hey I gotta go. I love and miss you all wish I was back on the beach in Mexico with you guys. :) Love Bryan

However, surprised we were to learn that the Marines would have to pay for their uniforms with their miserly salary, it was apparent that it was fine with Bryan. He had settled in well at boot camp and was actually having some fun times. I decided I would ignore the comments about the tattoo. We received his next letter on August 14.

Hey Family!

Well it's the start of a new week. Field week that is. Not really sure how it's going to be. Lots of walking around and field training. It will probably be hard but fun. We have the gas chamber :{ Not really scared of it but not looking forward to it. That is on Tuesday. The night fire will be fun. Tracer bullets are really cool. They are green and red and you can see it at night where your bullets are going. That's all I know about next week. I'll tell you how it goes next Sunday. Got your letters and your card dad. I had to open the card in front of the whole platoon. They got a kick out of the card. Well last week was firing week. I was an ammo recruit. That means I got up early and went to the range and got the ammo out of the Armory And took all the Ammo to the 200-yard line. Every day I got the ammo for 3 platoons. That is about 210 recruits and for 3 platoons we got 18,000 rounds of ammo a day. That is close to 90,000 rounds we shot off in a week. Well we qualified on Friday. That was pretty cool. There are 3 different ranks you can get. 1) is Marksman, which is the lowest 2) sharpshooter and 3) Expert. Our platoon won the range. We beat 5 other platoons overall. My personal score was 231 out of a possible 250 which is really good. The highest score was a 240 so I got Expert, I was pretty excited about that. At the 500-yard line I shot 8 out of 10 shots in the black. The black is the bullseye. That means I am better than an Army sniper. So, thanks for all your prayers they make my bullets fly true.

We had an 8-mile hike yesterday that was a pretty easy hike. My legs get chaffed. It hurt to walk but nothing that would stop me. I am so motivated. I just keep thinking about how we are almost done with boot camp!

Hey, keep praying and keep writing. They are so much of an encouragement. Our platoon is honor platoon for Mike Company. Mike Company is the BEST on base. So, we are the BEST of the BEST!

Hey, I got to go. I love you all and miss you a lot. Can't wait to see you. Love Bryan Chambers

Like clockwork another letter faithfully came from our very motivated Expert ranked recruit.

August 21, 2007

Hey family,

Well it was an interesting week. Field week. It was pretty cool. We got out flak jackets and helmets and learned how to fire with all our gear on. We learned how to use urban cover, like walls, rooftops and pipes. It was all right. We were pretty dirty. I probably had a pound of sand in my pockets. We also learned about face paint and camouflage. Not much happened this week, a few good stories but they would be impossible to write down. I have so much to tell you guys when I see you. Visitors Thursday I am looking forward to so much.

Hey, bring some Krispy Kreme donuts with you on that Thursday! That picture makes me smile and be very hungry every time I look at it. I enjoy all the pictures. Next week is Crucible week. I am really nervous about it. Scared of the unknown, I guess. We don't know much about it just that it's going to be a really big butt kicker. I have already packed all the food for the next 3 days. That is 3 MREs. 1 a day on the last day of the crucible we have a 12 mile hike up the hill they call the Reaper. They say it's really big and almost straight up. I have done 8 miles of the 12 and the 8 wasn't that bad so that's just 4 more miles from where we turned around. I'll just have to remember Hollie and my way of hiking. Pick a point and make it that point and picking another point. I think about you guys all the time.

Almost every chow I eat a lot of things I didn't use too. One is salad. Boy do I eat a lot of salad. Cream cheese and bagels hmmm. And the fact that peanut butter will go with and on anything, bananas, pancakes, cereal, apples. I would eat it plain. A spoon and a jar of peanut butter.

That's pretty good. I'll have to take Dad out for a greasy spoon breakfast because that is what I have basically every day.

Let's see, our platoon is now at 67 recruits. We started with 81. That is down quite a few recruits. For sure it will go down 1 more. Johnson Campbell has cellulitis. It is a cut that gets infected. It can get serious pretty quick. After this week is over, really all downhill from there. Just swim week, team week and that's it.

Hey about what we do for the 10 days…I could care less about where we are or what we do…we could drive around for that time. I just want to be with you guys. I would be happy just to sit on the couch with you guys. Just be with FAMILY! Oh and Dad, lots of food. I will spend 100 dollars on food! You can count on that! McDonald's, chips, pop, candy, peanut butter, bananas, oranges more

Little Debbies and junk food. I will try to clog an artery before I go to SOI!! (School of Infantry) Hey thanks for your prayers and your support. I pray for you guys too. Hey Dad, if you are still working installs for Home Depot in 4 years, I'll be your helper/ partner. I'll work for you as long as you want. I LOVE you all. I see you all in my dreams. The only dreams I have here are of you guys. I'll write to you later. Love Bryan

Bryan's letters revealed his love for his family and warmed our hearts. The offer to work for his dad when he had fulfilled his duties as a Marine was particularly tender. Indeed, the words our son shared about his dreams granted me a good reason to feel deeply blessed and to have a good cry. His letter showcased how hungry he was, awakening a longing in my mother's heart to prepare him a meal like in days far removed. As I read and re-read his letters, I discovered between the lines he wrote that even as our beloved recruit was transforming into a Marine, he was still just a boy missing his family and the way of life he had sacrificially left behind.

August 28

Hey family,

Well I think this is going to be a long letter. For a couple of reasons. 1) I just got done with the crucible and 2) I am doing my laundry, so I have a while to write.

Let's start with field week. I don't remember if I told you about the gas chamber? Well it was pretty bad :{ It was CX gas. It makes your body feel like it's on fire and when you breathe it in it takes your breath away. You can't breathe. Then snot and drool start to pour out of your nose and mouth. It was not very fun. I found out that Infantry has to do it 1 time every year. So that was in case I didn't tell you. Now onto crucible week. The Crucible was pretty tough. Just so exhausting. We walked with packs on for 3 days and did all these obstacles. Like carrying a victim. We carried a 190-pound guy for a mile, and we had 20 minutes to do it in. If you failed an obstacle you had to go drag Fred. Fred is a 170-pound dummy. You have to drag him a ways then come back. The food wasn't really a problem except for the lack of it. It made us all really weak. I saved 2 MREs for the last day so I had a good lunch and a dinner. We woke up and did the Reaper. It was hard but not that hard. I had a harder time on the hike back. When we got back to the squad bay we took a very quick shower and went and had The Warrior's breakfast. That's where we all stuffed ourselves for almost an hour. Boy were we all SICK because of all the food we ate! I twisted my ankle about 20 times on the Crucible, but I wasn't going to stop no matter what. I also have the worst rash on my privates. It hurts so bad I could hardly walk. It is slowly getting better but still hurts like getting needles stuck in that area. So this week is swim week 2.

I can't tell you how much I miss you guys and how much I just want to see your faces and hear your voices. OH, if you are wondering why this letter is crumpled up a DRILL INSTRUCTOR took it away. I thought I was

*going to have to write the whole letter again. I got to go.
I'll write you later. Love you all. Bryan*

We were so relieved that The Crucible was over! We were proud of our son. So proud! I was indeed aggravated at the Drill Instructor though! I would never receive the long letter he had intended to write.

Bryan wrote one of his final letters as a Recruit on Sunday September the 4th.

*Hey family,
Well the week has come and gone. I was told that 3rd phase goes by slow, but it is REALLY going slow. I don't know why. We are keeping pretty busy. We had swim every day until Friday. We had our Service outfits fitted for. I must say we look pretty good in the uniforms. The swim class were pretty cold. Not really hard. It goes from 4 being the easiest to 1 being the hardest. I passed 2 and didn't have the chance to try 1 but that's ok. I heard they almost drown you.*

On my birthday we did our Military IDs and a lot of drill getting ready for final drill. I almost made it through the whole day without a Drill Inspector knowing it was my birthday. On mail call they were looking at our IDs and DI Sgt. Liske noticed it was my birthday. I had to stand up and look down at the Quarter deck (which is where we get smoked) He said my birthday present was getting smoked. It's ok just makes me stronger.

We marched around the families that were here for India Company graduation. That made me happy but sad too. So close and yet so far away. I cannot wait to see you all. I am pretty sure you can and will be able to recognize me. I am still 160 pounds. We got weighed every weekend and I stayed 160 pounds the whole time. Even during the Crucible. Sounds like everyone will be pretty busy when I am home. Dad with work. Jen with the kids. Hollie with school. Hopefully I'll get to spend a lot of time with the whole family. I am looking forward to walks with Mom and Dog and whoever else tags along. Breakfast with Dad especially. I miss everyone. Jen and Isaiah and the kids. Sundays here are nice but kinda sad for me. Sunday afternoons were when Hollie and I hung out. I really miss that more than I ever thought I would. What they say is true. You don't know what you have till it's gone.

Thank you for all your letters. They are a really big Moral booster for me. I stay really motivated and try not to think about how much I miss you guys. Most of the time it doesn't work. I think about you all the time. I even dream about you guys. We have some guy in our platoon that will wake up screaming YES SIR! from the dreams he has. But for me it's a good way to wake up after having a dream with you guys in it. I wake up at least 5 times a night to use the head. What do you expect when you drink 80 ounces of water before you go to bed? I can get 3 water bowels down before I puke. That's almost 120 ounces! That's a lot of water! You should measure out 80 ounces and drink it in under 5 minutes. It's hard to say the least and it makes your stomach hurt.

I am looking forward to " Good Times " Hollie :) We have had a lot and will have a lot more. You can count on that. Just 2 weeks 4 days away! You just might have to play hooky from school. 18 days and a wake up. I got to go. Love you all SO MUCH!!!
Bryan

I purchased a green notebook binder and lovingly placed each of his letters in it. It was a valued treasure I took out and read when my mother's heart grew lonely, anxious and I needed to smile.

It's Graduation Day!

Granda, Bryan, Craig

Jennifer, Bryan, Hollie

Bryan's family during time he was at boot camp.

Chapter 3
DEPLOYMENT

After graduating from boot camp in September 2005, and a brief trip home, Bryan started the School of Infantry at Camp Pendleton in Southern California. He then moved across the parade deck to attend his MOS (Military Occupational Specialty) school where he was trained as a LAV (Light Armoured Vehicle) crewman. Following graduation from these schools Bryan was then stationed at Camp Lejeune in North Carolina. In the brief time between his move to the East Coast and deployment, we were able to visit him over the Easter holiday weekend at his base in North Carolina.

A few short months later, after a memorable family trip to Las Vegas complete with houseboating on Lake Meade, our beloved son would deploy with 2nd LAR BN Alpha Co 1st PLT to Iraq. He would embark on his journey amid countless prayers and petitions that he would remain safe and return to us. In an unexpected move moments before he left our home that August day, my son positioned me on the landing of our stairs. He said he needed to look me straight in the eyes. As the words left Bryan's mouth, I was stunned to realize the message actually came from my Father God. "Mother, don't lose your faith," he said, "I'm afraid you will lose your faith."

In shock, after searching his face, I surrendered speechless as I buried my face in his long embrace. It was in those moments I understood the testing of my faith would surely come.

His boots hit the ground on September 11, 2006, the anniversary of a very ominous day in US history.

As parents we busied ourselves with the routines of daily life. Craig kept himself occupied with an overloaded work schedule. I attempted to live normally, but nothing in my life was normal. I lived in a childless home, and my warrior child was a boot on the frontlines of the War in Iraq.

Autumn on the Western slope of Colorado was a delight to be explored. The crisp days grew shorter. The skies were beyond the bluest of blues and beckoned me outside. I soon found to my distress that I was hesitant to leave home. What if I missed a call from my son? Each morning I would instantly awake at three A.M. without the aid of an alarm clock. I would slip quietly down stairs to my favorite chair. There I would open the Word of Life and gather strength for the new day. I would study the Word of God and pour out my heart to my Father through the journaling of my prayers.

I had become deeply burdened by the hardness of heart I had observed and sensed that was slowly creeping into my son's personality since he had entered the Marine Corps. I wondered at the cause and remembered how aghast I was when I saw he slept with a baseball bat by his bed at Camp Lejeune. Was that reason for this hardness and disillusionment? What had happened there? I was dismayed and tearful at the daily, relentless fear that threatened my peace since his deployment. During those sacred hours, the Spirit of God reassured me through the study of His word that His love for my son was greater than I could possibly comprehend. Bryan belonged to Him and he was safe in His care even if that resulted in a place of suffering.

It was a hard message for a mother who loved hard to receive. I reminded myself of God's character and all the ways He had proven Himself faithful in the past. Hadn't He heard and responded to my impassioned cry for a Father all those long years ago? He had become my personal Savior through my belief in His Son Jesus Christ and had carried me through personal trauma. His healing love had given me security and as I followed His leading, He had introduced me to my husband. God's presence had been tangible in our family's history through an abundance of trials already. I wept as I remembered His gracious response to the pleas He heard for Bryan's life at his birth.

I had no doubt in my Sovereign God. The fathomless issue of God's sovereignty had been explained to me in ordinary simple conversations of life when I was still a young child.

The grace of God reached out to me through the love and caring of a young pastor and his wife. This special man of God and his wife committed to drive across town to take my single mother and her children to church every Sunday morning like clockwork. He would return to get us once again on Sunday evening. On these special outings, he would disciple us in the ways and the loving character of a God who had mercy on each of us. I embraced this marvelous God with the grasp of a child who had been drowning in a sea of hopelessness, and I never let go.

Using scripture that pastor explained that God was good and without equal. He was the King of kings and the Lord of lords. He had no beginning and He has no end. He is outside of time. He is the ruler of everything. He has no limitations. He has a master plan explained in the Holy Scriptures and a purpose for our individual lives. This amazing God is all-knowing, and nothing is outside His control.

He went on to tell us that even if this sovereign God were to allow the unthinkable to take place and we find it repulsive, we should be careful not to call Him into judgment. He explained that God's sovereignty meant that there is nothing entering our lives that God did not decree or allow. He said if we were willing to trust Him there is nothing He would not work out for our good.

As I thought back on these teachings of scripture and the years that I had lived in this troubled yet beautifully endowed world, I knew these truths to be verifiable in intimate ways. No, I had no doubt in my sovereign God. My doubts were founded in myself.

I knew that to follow and surrender to the biblical God was to purposely give Him the reins of control over my life. This decision felt unsafe for one who had a tendency to insist on personal protection and on plotting a safer route. I had already experienced some dreadful, stormy adventures in life, and I readily admit to a preference of living life in a controlled climate. Yes, from now on I wanted my skies to be nothing but blue. I had no desire to go through additional trials. I wanted to forgo testing, or at the very least choose the test. Given a choice, I would select one that would not have anything to do with my kids. Still I had learned through living that it was in the bona fide testing of my faith that the beliefs I thought I possessed would be proven genuine.

Could I do this? Could I do what God might require of me? Would I forfeit my faith if God allowed something to happen to my son? Would I do an about face? Or would I continue to trust Him? I wanted to shout, "Yes I will!" but would I? I recalled the struggles of great heroes in the Bible like the Apostle Peter. Even he denied knowing the Lord Jesus when he feared for his own life. Not just once but three times! And then there was Thomas who was one of the twelve disciples. He became filled with doubts to the point he could no longer believe unless he saw with his physical eyes and touched with his fingers the object of his faith. I was no hero. I was just a mom. I fell silent in my heart. Could I lose my faith? Was that even *possible?* And if it was possible, did that mean I wasn't secure in Christ? Those were just a few haunting questions I asked of myself. I wrestled with my thoughts to settle these dilemmas in my mind. I had no answers.

Slowly I permitted myself to work outside in my flower gardens. I took morning walks with Kailey, Bryan's golden retriever. I drew strength by going to work with my husband. I drank in the peaceful beauty around us as he installed doors and windows in some of the most beautiful areas in our mountainous region. It was a common blessing for us to go to Telluride, Ouray, Gunnison, Montrose, Lake City, Crested Butte. Even Aspen and Glenwood Springs. We prayed often for our son and he was ever in our thoughts and conversations. Evenings, weekends, and days, I was surrounded by my daughter Jennifer and my four beautiful grandchildren. They were in varying stages from helpless infant to audacious toddlerhood. This sweet family lived a short block away and filled my life with so much delight. I was blessed to be able to frequently see my daughter Hollie Mae who lived a manageable forty-five-minute drive away in Grand Junction. Tuesday nights continued as they had for years. Cherished ladies came to my home for Bible study at 6:30 and stayed till 10 and longer. During those hours of fellowship, we would sample desserts, have concerts of praise and open our Bibles and our hearts to each other. As we studied scripture through Bible studies, we were reminded that we live in a fallen world where suffering is a part of the human experience. Suffering could either draw us to God, or we could allow it to drive us from Him in distrust. We embraced the sorrows and delights in each other's lives and believed God to show Himself a personal God to each of us. These special friends had watched Bryan grow and had embraced him as their very own. They prayed for his safety and were some of his biggest fans.

Our family practiced prayer as a way of life. We were not hesitant to enlist everyone we knew to pray for him. He had prayer warriors in Colorado, Indiana, Texas, Tennessee, Illinois, and New Mexico. I had enlisted a group of extraordinary people to pray and fast for our son. Each took a day of the week to pray for him. This continued the entire time he was in Iraq. I grew insistently desperate that believers would pray for my son. I discerned with increasing certainty that what God had shown me in that vision years ago would surely come to pass. The only thing I was uncertain of was when our day of trouble would come.

In October, the shocking news came that Bryan's Lieutenant had stepped on an IED (improvised explosive device) concealed below the ground's surface. Bryan and his unit had been patrolling a small city on foot during the previous days. At the last minute on this specific day the Lieutenant instructed Bryan to stay behind and work on his

LAV (Light Armoured Vehicle) instead of going on the patrol. The Lieutenant's injuries were grave and sent him stateside. On Christmas Day I received a breathless call from Bryan.

His foot patrol had endured yet another IED blast. They were celebrating survival with a victory cigar. It had become a tradition. With this news we poured out our thanksgiving to God for His watchful protection and continued our prayers for our son and his band of brothers with ever growing passion.

Soon it was January. Our scheduled business trip to Texas came as a welcomed diversion from the marking off calendar days till our beloved son would be stateside again. Driving home through the beautiful Sangre de Cristo Mountains, Craig and I received a call from Bryan on our cell phone. It was comforting to hear his voice. It was a kindness of the Spirit who sent a gentle reminder to my troubled mind that He could connect us with our son no matter where either of us wandered.

It was during this trip that I was impressed to memorize specific scripture. The voice in my mind that I recognized as the Spirit of God urged me to memorize Psalm 103. It was January 13, 2007. Instinctually I knew I was being prepared for coming events. Quickly I turned to the passage in scripture and embraced the hope within. The verses taught me of the benefits of knowing and praising God. He forgives all our sins I read. He heals all our diseases. He redeems our lives from the pit. He crowns us with love and compassion, and He satisfies our desires with good things so that our youth is renewed like the eagles! As I continued to read the following verses, I was overcome with the vastness of his provision and concern for His own. My heart recalled again the vision God had shown me at Bryan's birth all those fleeting years before. The Spirit was gracious to write the Psalm quickly on my trembling heart. As the time drew closer to the day he would be out of the "sand box" and off the battlefield, I experienced increasing peace. I reasoned within myself that I had been praying that God would change the plan. "Oh Father!" my heart pleaded, "There has to be another way! Please change the plan!" Perhaps He had a plan B.

Bryan called home on Sunday, February 25, 2007. He was one last mission away from finishing his first deployment. Our conversation was full of combined joy and rejoicing over his scheduled homecoming. In the stillness of special moments, he confessed to me that God was speaking to him while he was on post. It was there in those long, quiet, sobering hours of dark solitude that the Spirit was changing his hard heart through personal dialogue with God. He said he was grateful for his time in Iraq. That had not been the case before. As he recounted the times he had survived attacks from the cowardly enemy, he expressed how thankful he was to be alive. In his final moments on the phone my tenderhearted child heard the unshed tears in my voice. "Mom, do not worry." He urged gently. "You will not hear from me for several days." He cautioned me, "I will call when I can." His voice grew tender, "Mom, it's all going to be okay. I love you Mom". In the space of a whisper the satellite moved. His voice faded. He was gone. That night my heart was full. It overflowed with gratefulness and splashed hope all over my troubled mind. I was grateful that my son was on speaking terms with God. I knew he had been hardened to the ways of God for a time. What he had confessed to me during those deeply intimate last moments gave rest to my own troubled soul and gave me much to talk over with the Father during the watches of the night. The next couple of days were spent happily contemplating his homecoming. We put the finishing touches on his bedroom and waited on Bryan's call.

Climbing under the covers on Tuesday February 27, 2007, I exchanged fear for faith and gave Bryan into God's care once again. As I released the panic that often sought me in the darkness of night, I felt cradled in the comforting arms of God. For the first time since he deployed, I laid down and slept, without waking, in deep complete sleep.

During this time of deep rest, horrific events were unfolding on the other side of the world. There in the heat of the day, along the riverbanks of the ancient Euphrates River, twenty-year-old Lance Corporal Bryan Chambers drove his Light Armored Vehicle over an IED buried deep below the surface. In that moment of time, my warrior child was catapulted into the mysterious and hidden ways of God.

Chapter 4
THE CALL

My morning arrived unlike any other since my son deployed to Iraq. Astonishingly, I awoke completely refreshed. Unwilling to peel back the covers on that crisp, cold, bright winter morning, I pulled the comforter close and snuggled deeper into its downy warmth. I marveled at the lateness of the hour as I struggled to read the clock. I had slept ALL night! As I lay there beholding the stark beauty of naked tree limbs reaching toward the glorious new morning, I gave thanks to my heavenly Father for his kindness to give me a much-needed rest. Quickly my thoughts returned to the last conversation I had had with our son.

"I'll call you, Mom!" he said. "When I get back from the mission, I'll call you!"

I quickly calculated that it had barely been three days since the mission began, so it was unlikely I would hear from him that day. I smiled at the thought of his youthful delight in the prospect of coming home. How wonderful it would be to have our boy safely home in small town Delta, Colorado!

As I anticipated the day ahead, I finally threw back the covers and went in search of Craig. My husband had set aside a full day for me! A honey-do day! A honey I'll go and do whatever you desire day! With delight I found him in his favorite place cooking a man-sized breakfast. My generous husband set his breakfast before me and cooked himself another. Such a dear. It was going to be a great day! Now, if I should receive that call from Bryan, it would be a picture-perfect day! That anticipated call did not come. In its place came a call no parent could ever be prepared for.

Craig and I stood in the upstairs hallway outside Bryan's bedroom. With great satisfaction we surveyed the progress we had made on his room. Gone was the simple twin sized bed where he had slept since boyhood. In its place stood a massive log bed befitting the man he had become. Busily unwrapping the new bed linens, my thoughts wandered to days far removed. I had loved being a boy's mom. What would he be like when he returned, this sudden man child of mine?

The ring of the phone interrupted my fond musings. Reluctantly putting aside days long gone, I reached for the phone.

"Hello. This is Granda. May I help you?" I asked.

I could hear paper rustling and faint muffled voices in the background. "Great!" I thought. "A telemarketer at ten o'clock in the morning!"

"Granda?" a man's voice asked.

"Yes." I replied with a sigh.

"Granda Chambers, Bryan's mom?" he queried.

The simple mention of my child's name garnered the voice on the other end of the line my full attention. I became focused. "Yes." I confirmed quickly.

"Ma'am...this is Gunnery Sergeant Ottie of the United States Marine Corps."

I detected a reluctance in his voice. "Yes..." I said with cautious hesitancy.

"Ma'am." My mind instantly registered the shift of tone in his voice.

"Ma'am, I regret to inform you that as of approximately twelve o'clock p.m. February 28, Iraqi time, your son became a casualty of war."

My body went still. My brain scrambled to comprehend what I had just been told. In those dreadful moments of time, I knew our day of trouble had arrived. My inner soul began calling out for my God to help me. "Oh my God! Oh my God! Please help me! I need you! Please help me!" I turned to myself as I checked my thoughts. "How could you not know? You should have known." I scolded myself harshly.

I quickly calculated that it would have been around 4 a.m. Colorado time. I should have been praying...I was sleeping. I felt a sense of shame.

"Oh," I managed to whisper out loud.

My only son was dead. He was so young. Twenty years was such a short time. The memories of his birth came rushing forth. I had chosen to give this child to God. He had every right to exercise His ownership and call him home. When I had finally said "Okay" to God, Gunney thought I was talking to him.

Thoughts swirled around my head and bumped one into another as I sought to bring order to my chaotic thoughts. "Weren't they supposed to come to my door to tell me my son was dead?" I asked myself. "Instead they call me on a phone??" I was offended.

As the reality of the moment began to seep its way into my body, I needed to say something, but I was frozen in the pain of stunned silence. "The van! Was the van with a Marine dressed in his blues coming to my house?" I asked myself. In my mind I struggled with what the protocol was to be. "Were they outside already?" I questioned internally.

I glanced past Craig through the view of an open window to check. "How DARE they call me on a telephone and give me such life-altering news?" I continued my internal rambling. "The Marine Corps should have handled this properly!" I was suddenly intensely angry at this Gunnery Sergeant. "Oh, Father, you HAVE to help me!!" I inwardly raged. I opened my mouth to speak but despite labored effort no sound came. Tears began to blur my vision. Sorrow ran wet down my face as I surrendered the anger and acknowledged the truth. My son was dead.

"Ma'am?" Gunney said with uncertainty, "Ma'am, have you heard from Bryan today?"

His astonishing question instantly loosened my dumbstruck tongue.

"Nooo…?" I said with a sudden burst of voice and confusion. My thoughts were bouncing off the sides of my brain like a metal ball in a pinball machine.

"How could I hear from him if he was a casualty??" I asked myself. "Doesn't that mean he's dead??" My mind immediately did a word search. "How could I not know the definition of causality?" I asked myself with incredibility. *Maybe there is another meaning to the word?!"*

In a millisecond the Lord of hope both gripped and shook me.

"Is Bryan alive?!!" I asked God passionately. "Oh God is he alive??" My heart pounded in my ears. "Please let him be alive!! Oh, please, let him be alive!" I pleaded with God as I internally jumped up and down.

"Ma'am, I'm sure you will hear from him today," Gunney offered.

"Okay…" I barely whispered, looking wild-eyed at my husband trying to communicate with him despite being mute. For all that was sacred and dear to me the only word I seemed to be able to articulate was *okay*. And it was !! Was my son dead or was my son alive??

Gunney broke the deafening silence. "Ma'am the only information I have other than what I have told you is," he paused reading from the rustling paper, "something has happened to his leg."

"Okay…" I repeated yet again as I groaned within. I tried to slow down my thoughts and embrace the meaning behind his words. I didn't have time to talk to Gunney when it was the Lord I wanted to question.

"Lord, what *is* this?" I begged silently. "What is happening? Something is wrong with his *leg*?? I inquired specifically of the Lord. "Something is wrong with Bryan's leg?!" In my mind, our son went from being dead to possibly being alive in moments. Hope began to rise amidst turmoil as my heart pounded and vision darkened. Still I said nothing to Gunney.

"Mrs. Chambers you can ask me *any* question you want," he offered. Though I intently tried to speak I was struck dumb. "I will attempt to answer your questions," he added sympathetically.

"Okay," I finally whispered yet again.

"You can call me back anytime," he offered. "You can call as many times as you want. (He was at a loss as to what to say.) I will repeat to you all that I have told you," he added. He waited uneasily. "I'm sure you will hear from Bryan soon," he comforted as I began to melt audibly.

As I slowly slid down the wall to make the carpet my chair, I struggled with great difficulty to find my voice. Craig stood ready to take the phone. I uttered my first full sentence during the entire exchange. "Would you," my voice broke, "Would you please … repeat to my husband … everything you … " I softly choked out, "everything you just told me? He's on his way downstairs to get on the second line."

I sank fully to the floor clinging to the telephone as if it were a lifeline to my son. I couldn't hand over the phone. I couldn't hang up. I *WOULDN'T* hang up! Maybe if I stayed on the line, the information he would tell my husband would somehow be different? Maybe I didn't hear correctly? Maybe Gunney would admit it was all an awful mistake and Bryan was not at all hurt. Maybe. I was grasping for a different outcome.

I was brought back to reality when I heard Gunnery Sergeant Ottie talk to the father of my only son. Again, I heard the grim phrase "casualty of war." The weight of the phone became too heavy to hold. Slowly it slipped out of my hands. The frozen dam burst with force as my silence was shattered. Dropping face first into the carpet fibers, I emptied the groans of my wounded mind and heart as I cried out fiercely for my son.

As if being lifted from a deep fog, I felt my husband gently gather me into his arms. With tears from his eyes spilling onto my face and neck, we huddled on the floor.

In that moment all else faded away and that soggy, tear drenched carpet became an altar of prayer and sacrifice. Together we cried for our son's life.

Chapter 5
SEEKING BRYAN

Somewhere amid physical shock, free falling tears, and impassioned prayers arose the belief that our all-wise, personal God was watching over our precious son and would return him to our family. Drawing from an unmined source of God's grace, Craig and I gathered strength to help each other stand and walk down the stairs into an uncertain future together.

We broke the alarming news to his sisters with great gentleness and very tender hearts. Straightaway we were gripped with a sense of pressing urgency that demanded immediate intercession for Bryan. Jennifer came quickly to be with us with our precious grandchildren ages 9 months to 3½ years, in tow. Hollie Mae was attending Mesa State in Grand Junction, Colorado. It was a school day. Later that night she would be working at Red Robin. The settled plan was to let her know if we heard any further news about her brother's condition. In the meantime, she would maintain her schedule and pray where she was.

I quickly recognized the tender workings of the Spirit evidenced by the very presence of Craig at my side when I received the call. In the course of ordinary life, he would have been many hours away from home and possibly out of cell coverage. Craig rapidly cleared his work schedule with one call, and we became inseparable. Together we became focused on our son. We anxiously awaited news from Bryan and the Marine Corps. We knelt together in prayer around the coffee table then settled in the living room and softly cried into our tissues as we waited. We talked of our faith in God as we felt His presence with us. We comforted one another with biblical truth. We listened to music that reinforced our belief and faith in God and fixed our anxious hearts on hope.

I loaded the CD player with praise music from my Bible studies. One praise song after another filled the air reminding us that even now, especially now. . . God was worthy of our worship. Craig's ringtone interrupted our reflections. It was Chris Tomlin's version of *Everlasting God.* The tune beckoned me to find and play the CD. The lyrics rang out eternal truth as the song played over and over.

Strength will rise as we wait upon the Lord.
We will wait upon the Lord.
We will wait upon the Lord.
Strength will rise as we wait upon the Lord.
We will wait upon the Lord.
We will wait upon the Lord.
Our God You reign forever
Our hope, our strong Deliverer
You are the everlasting God
The everlasting God
You do not faint
You won't grow weary
You're the defender of the weak
You comfort those in need
You lift us up on wings like eagles
Our God, you reign forever
Our hope, our Strong Deliverer
You are the everlasting God
The everlasting God

Everlasting God, Brenton Brown, Ken Riley[1]

The Holy Spirit spoke to our hearts through every word of this song. It became our anthem. Our orders were clear. We were to wait on Him. We were to remember who He was. He was the Everlasting God!

Though we were in danger of fainting and becoming weary, He wasn't nor ever would be. He was the defender of the weak. Having been severely injured, we knew our Bryan was so weak. God would defend and watch over our son. He comforts those in need. Our son needed His comfort. We needed His comfort. So great was this need it had the potential to crush us under its weight. We needed an eternal perspective of this very personal invitation to pain and suffering. God would lift us up on wings like eagles and allow us to see a bigger picture. He was our God, our hope our Strong Deliverer. We each had invested in a personal relationship with Him. We knew Him.

As the day stretched long into the early evening hours, we continued to cry out on Bryan's behalf. We did not doubt that God was at work. We trusted that He would grant us strength and faith to believe Him no matter the outcome. We prayed that we would hear from Bryan soon. As the night turned ever darker, I voiced what had become clearer with each passing hour. "Craig," I choked out with sudden clarity. "I know Bryan would have called us by now!" A hush fell over those present. "He can't call!" I cried with sudden alarming comprehension. "He's not able to!!"

I trembled with the sure knowledge I had been given. It was much more than a broken leg. Forcing my panic-stricken emotions under control and my brain to function, I promptly recalled that the military used a hospital in Landstuhl, Germany. Marines and soldiers serving in Iraq and Afghanistan would be transported there when their injuries were severe. Pushing aside mounting alarm I got on the computer and located the phone number to the hospital. Hovering near Craig's side as he dialed Germany, I prayed that he would get a connection to the hospital. I breathed audible prayers of thanksgiving and elation when in the space of a few seconds Craig was talking to the operator at the hospital. My husband had a calmness that was unearthly. He explained that our son had been injured on the battlefield in Iraq. He inquired if they had a Lance Corporal Bryan Chambers as a patient.

Quickly the patient list was checked. Bryan's name was not on it. The voice on the other side of the world compassionately offered to check the flight manifest list. She clarified that while the hospital was not an official military hospital as we had believed, it was where the military brought their wounded. The hospital staff knew in advance if wounded military personnel would be on the next incoming medevac flight. Bryan's name was not on that list either. Craig was invited to call back in a few hours to check the updated flight list.

Our intercessions intensified around the clock. Prayer support grew as we urgently reached out to others. We contacted our extended family and life-long friends. We reached out in desperation to all the churches where we had ever been members. I invited Marine Parents.com, an online support group I had been impressed to join just *days* before, to pray for our son. We were desperate for God to answer our cries for his life. Soon hundreds of people were praying for our son. I was overcome with thankfulness for the body of Christ and their willingness to intercede on behalf of Bryan.

The tears of a thankful heart mixed with grief would not cease. Beyond asking God to spare our son's life, grant wisdom to the doctors and heal his leg, we couldn't pray without more specific detail of his injuries. We needed information about his current condition in real time. Behind the scene, God was at work arranging a direct line for us to get a first-hand accounting of the injuries our beloved child had suffered. Though miles away, bound by a kindred spirit of heart, my dear friend Carolyn was also seeking God's face for more information on Bryan's injuries. As she prepared to come to me, I poured out my heart to her on the phone. "Certainly someone, somewhere knows where my son is?!!" I agonized. In those moments Carolyn was reminded of a Colorado friend who had a son in the Navy. He too had been deployed to Iraq. Was it too much to *believe* that he might know something about our son's physical condition?

Within a short period of time we received news that the Navy mom had sent an urgent email to her son. She inquired if he knew anything about a young, injured Lance Corporal Bryan Chambers from Colorado. We were wonderstruck at the fingerprints of God. This unknown son had direct knowledge of our son! How like our God to speedily answer our prayer! Someone somewhere *did* indeed know something about our son!! Our hearts absorbed the information God provided like parched, barren land soaking up life-giving rain.

The correspondence we received was the answer to the specifics we had prayed for, but the fruit it bore was painfully bitter. The information came in the form of an email from the Navy mom's son. Not only was he a doctor, he was THE Medical Officer for 2nd LAR (Light Armored Reconnaissance) Battalion. Bryan's very own battalion!

It was March 1, 2007. The time was 9:30 on a Thursday morning. It was just short of twenty-four hours since I had answered the call that had up-ended our world. All these agonizing hours later the Marine Corps still knew nothing of his condition.

Our Sovereign God had intimate details. In His mercy He provided us with a fresh accounting. The detailed list of war's assault on our son's physical body was brutal. We read, and as our eyes tripped over the words, re-read again. Our hearts imploded and tears blinded our eyes. Words faded in and out on the screen. With trembling bodies and pounding hearts, we stared at the computer, trying to comprehend the extent of Bryan's injuries. The devastating rapid succession of the bullet points regarding our son's physical condition was in real time. It took my breath away in torment and brought me immediately to my knees in prayer.

The Medical Officer informed us that he had just gotten off the phone with Balad ICU in Iraq where our son was currently being assessed and treated. He explained that Bryan was intubated (he had a breathing tube in his throat). He had a machine assisting his breathing and was in a sleep like state with no movement. We were informed that he had suffered a broken right lower leg. Both bones, the tibia and fibula, were fractured as a result of the IED blast. Orthopedists in Al Asad (his first stop) had been able to place pins in his leg to set the bones. An artery in his lower leg had been cut as a result of the trauma. The surgeons had hoped the bleeding would stop, but it had not. That very morning our son was taken back into the operating room.

We were informed that the bleeding vessel was embolized and that his right foot had good color and a strong pulse. The strong pulse in his lower extremity resulted in the decision that his limb would remain intact and attached at the present time. My altered world tilted and began a slow spin. I groaned with prayers. "Oh, Lord Jesus, please help Bryan!" I pleaded internally. "Please help us!"

The possibility that Bryan could lose his lower leg was hard to fathom. We paused to cry out to our God for ability to comprehend what we had just read. Our shocked minds were slow in understanding. We prayed for calmness and courage to continue to read the lengthy email.

We read that during the procedure to fix Bryan's fractured leg he also underwent an exploratory surgery of his abdomen. They uncovered bleeding in his abdomen from his spleen that had been lacerated. His spleen had been removed as a result. In my mind's eye I could visualize teams of surgeons working on his body trying to save his precious life. I prayed fervently for them. I asked the God who heals to guide their gifted hands.

They had found no other evidence of internal organ damage in the brief time he was at Al Asad. Immediately upon arrival at his next stop in Balad, he underwent another repeat explorative surgery to reassess his organs and view the spleen removal sight for stability. His abdomen was washed out.

My shocked mind grasped at a mental image. It came up blank as numbness started to creep into my mind. I vigorously shook my head to prevent myself from fainting and forced myself to continue to read the email. I felt another wave of shock wash over my soul, like an unexpected plunge into an arctic abyss.

The words on the computer screen told me that my son had severe scrotal bruising. Unmercifully, in letters of black, they pronounced that his right testicle had been removed. The remaining testicle was badly bruised. I felt my heart tear open at the possible unthinkable loss of future generations of grandbabies to cherish. The stated goal was to transport him to Landstuhl, Germany as soon as his oxygen needs met transportable levels. With great difficulty I tried to understand what that meant. Was he having difficulty absorbing oxygen? Wouldn't that be addressed by the breathing machine? I had so many questions I found myself voicing them aloud. We were also informed that he had been receiving blood transfusions.

The enormity of the onslaught of information was unbearable to process in one reading and required reading multiple times. Quickly we endeavored to send out an updated email to the community of believers praying for our warrior child. The remainder of that Thursday was spent in urgent specific prayer as we studied the email. Each of us played secretary to our own cell phones as Craig's ringtone reminded us frequently of our Everlasting God. Friends and neighbors sent expressions of hope as news spread through our hometown of Delta, Colorado.

Much later that day the Marine Corps finally called us back. They regretted that they still did not know anything more about our son or his injuries. Imagine how incredulous Gunnery Sergeant was when I gave him the full run down on Bryan's injuries!

"Where did you get this information!?" Gunnery Sergeant was incredulous. "We are the first line in the information chain! We don't have this information!" he said forcefully.

I told him of God's awe-inspiring intervention. "Sir, we believe in a God who answers prayer." I explained boldly, full of faith. "We prayed that God would connect us with whomever had information about our son's injuries. We needed to pray with specific detail for our son. What we've witnessed is the unseen hand of God at work." I recounted to him the connection I had with my friend Carolyn. I told of Carolyn's connection to the Navy mom. The astounded

Gunney slowly and silently processed the information. After moments of stunned silence he asked for the name of the Medical Officer and quickly asked if we would forward the email we had received. He requested to be included in the information loop. Before he got off the phone, he assured me his thoughts and prayers were with Bryan and our family.

Every few hours, like clockwork, my husband called Germany to check on the flight manifest list. Craig's enduring persistence was finally rewarded. Lance Corporal Bryan Chambers of the United States Marine Corps was on the next incoming flight to Germany.

We fell to our knees in thanksgiving and praise to God as we cheered Bryan on to his next stop. Our son was scheduled to arrive at Landstuhl Regional Medical Center in Landstuhl, Germany at 1:00 a.m. March 2, Colorado time. We had found Bryan! Our son was alive!

---

[1]Brown, Brenton, Riley, Ken, Everlasting God, Thankyou Music, Worldwide at Capitol CMG Publishing

Chapter 6
THE COST OF FREEDOM

The 2nd LAR Battalion to which our son was assigned
is a fast and mobilized armoured terrestrial reconnaissance
battalion of the United States Marine Corps. It is comprised
of H & S Co., (Headquarters and Supply Company), Alpha
Co., Bravo Co., Charlie Co., Delta Co., and Echo Co. Their
primary weapon system is the LAV-25. The LAV-25 is an
eight-wheeled, 13-ton, all-terrain, all-weather vehicle with
night capabilities. It provides strategic mobility to reach and
engage the threat and to conduct security recon and screening
missions. It is equipped with weapons and ammunition.

On February 28, 2007, Lance Corporal Bryan Chambers
was the lead driver of the Alpha Company LAV (light armoured
vehicle) convoy supporting combat operations in Al Anbar
province, Iraq. As the twenty-year-old Lance Corporal blazed
the trail ahead on mission, his vehicle ran over an Improvised
Explosive Device buried many feet below the surface. In the
immediate explosion, Bryan's vehicle commander Sgt. Chad

M. Allen paid the ultimate price. He was killed instantly. Three other Marines were wounded as they were ejected by the massive explosion that created a huge crater, toppled overhead power lines and propelled the entire engine block over 45 feet from the vehicle.

Bryan alone remained trapped in the crumpled remains of the smoldering wreckage of his LAV. Expecting the volatile cargo of 200 High Explosive Rounds and 100 armour penetrating rounds to catch fire and explode, orders came down the chain of command to leave the Lance Corporal and fall back. Braving imminent harm by entering the forty-five-yard killing zone created by the blast, two of his Marine brothers returned and fought courageously to free him with great difficulty from his fiery grave.

Miraculously the ammunition never caught fire despite the gravity of the explosion that turned the 13-ton eight-wheeled amphibious vehicle into twisted metal.

Having spent precious minutes repeatedly jumping on Bryan's femur in a distressing effort to free him from the wreckage, Bryan's brothers were racing against time. After an unsuccessful attempt to trache him, they applied tourniquets to his obvious injuries and rushed his lifeless body toward the incoming medevac helicopter. In the cramped cabin of a Black Hawk, the medic pumped Bryan's chest to keep the blood circulating till he could establish a heartbeat. The medic concentrated on giving the young Marine all the help he could as a buddy held Bryan's hand and shouted his name. They tried not to think of the probable outcome.

By the time the Black Hawk landed at the Al Asad Air Base in Al Anbar Province, their young Marine brother had not been breathing for an extended period. He had lost at least half of his blood volume and was still bleeding out from a huge scalp wound, a severely injured right leg and foot and from shrapnel inside his belly. Bryan was rushed back to the OR where the medical team trached him successfully and started pumping him with oxygen and life-giving blood.

The surgeons' hands were full as they raced against time to find and stop the bleeding from multiple sources. The anesthesiologist was frantically working to catch up with the immense blood loss and turn the crimson tide. By the time they had finished the initial surgery, the young Lance Corporal had taken in an unbelievable 30 units of blood! This is astounding as an adult human body only holds between 8 to 12 units of blood. The excessive amount bore witness to the fact that the injured Marine had shed his entire life's blood as he honored his duty to his country. He was bleeding out faster than the surgeons could repair and stop the flow. Most of the blood ended up in the suction and on the floor of the operating room. Still the surgeons and anesthesiologist worked relentlessly without reprieve.

The need for this massive amount of blood necessitated the use of walking donors. Emotions and pride overwhelmed the surgeons when their urgent cry went out over the loudspeakers for blood donors to come to the aid of their gravely injured comrade.

The men and women who lined up to answer the call were visually passionate and willing to give in the fight to save this young Marine's life. This system of blood donation, called the Walking Blood Bank, gives warm whole blood that accomplishes everything necessary. It carries oxygen, fills up empty vessels and helps the surgeon by forming a clot to stop the bleeding. The blood goes from donor to the patient in a matter of minutes. The use of the Walking Blood Bank was the young Marine's only hope as the supply of blood products available was limited at the war's frontline. The use of fresh whole blood has been virtually eliminated from transfusion medicine except in battlefield surgery. Diseases carried in the general population are too numerous and it's too impractical and expensive to execute. On the battlefield there is a different set of rules.

In the field hospital the surgeons were willing to accept a 1 in 5000 chance that the gravely injured Marine might get hepatitis when otherwise he had a 1 in 1 chance of dying from blood loss!

The Marine had a ruptured spleen, a severely injured right foot, a right femur fracture, a fractured jaw, severe scalp and face lacerations, a damaged right kidney, and a testicle that ended up not surviving.

Marines, soldiers and a few Air Force personnel stood in line to donate their own life blood for their fellow brother-in-arms. The Lance Corporal received 7 RBC (Red Blood Cells) units by donors from back home and 23 whole blood units from people there in Al Asad.

As the surgeons packaged up their brother for the helicopter ride to Balad ICU the anesthesiologist who had been with him the entire time studied his Colorado driver's license picture. The young Marine was probably 18 at the time it was taken. He had the biggest grin on his freckled boyish face. The Marine that left there was no longer a boy. He was a decorated veteran who stood shoulder to shoulder with the heroes of wars past.

During the debrief of the young Marine's case, there was elation among the military medicine warriors. They all agreed that saving this particular mother's son was like coming back from a 50- point deficit at halftime, kicking a winning field goal in overtime to win the football game. It was a spectacular save! John Elway would have been proud. The critically injured Marine's next stop was at the Air Force Theater Hospital in Balad, Iraq. He arrived aboard a Blackhawk helicopter.

The sound of the trauma alert sent nurses and orderlies dashing for the door that led to the helipad. The gurney crew hustled out to the chopper to receive their latest war casualty. The helicopter medics bundled him out on a gurney with speed. The nurses and orderlies followed the helicopter medics, who were pushing the gurney down the helipad. Their latest casualty entered the tent hospital under a giant US flag canopy named Hero's Highway. The young Lance Corporal was immediately swept into a small soft-wall setting of a tent hospital unit.

The ceiling height was approximately 7 feet. Bars and lights fixtures were suspended from the ceiling. It was there in that close intimate surrounding that these military medical warriors would work urgently on their young Marine and his critical medical care. With focused passion they spent themselves to keep a young American hero alive. It would take an additional three days in ICU and three more surgeries before this critically injured hero would be stable enough to be transported to his third stop on his journey home to America.

Chapter 7
ONE STOP FROM HOME

Bryan arrived in Landstuhl aboard one of the C-17s that ferry the injured from Iraq to Germany. He was cocooned in a modified body bag called a "hot pocket" that trapped his body heat inside. This ensured the critical warmth he needed during the five- hour transport from the hospital in Balad, Iraq.

Our war-torn son had been at the hospital in Germany for an hour when a call came from his father in the United States. It was Friday, March 2, at 4:30 a.m. Colorado time. The doctor quickly gave my husband Craig a head to toe assessment of our son which included an additional set of traumatic injuries.

His preliminary neurological exam appeared to be okay. He did note that Bryan had a small brain contusion. He had facial lacerations and a fractured jaw. He had arrived with chest tubes due to low oxygen levels in his blood. The doctor was hopeful that the tubes would be removed when Bryan was taken into surgery that afternoon. Dr. Sutherlin said our son's abdominal cavity was still open and would be cleaned out yet again. He was hopeful that the surgeons would be able to close it up afterwards. The doctor informed us that Bryan had a pelvic fracture. We added that information to the growing list of injuries he had sustained.

We were amazed and beyond humbled that he was still alive. Clearly God was sustaining his life. Dr Sutherlin gave us additional information about our son's right leg that had been fractured. Bryan's leg had suffered major bone damage above the knee in addition to the tibia and fibula breaks we were already aware of. He described our son's right foot as being very mangled. We were informed that the surgeons would reassess his right foot during the surgery and if the blood flow had stopped, they would remove it. In Dr. Sutherlin's rundown of Bryan's injuries, we learned our son's left foot had been peppered with small open wounds. The doctor further clarified that they would be taking him down to do a complete MRI before surgery. We were assured that he would call us with an update on our son as the day progressed.

Once again, we clung to each other and cried out to our God as we were held together by hope. Our child was so hurt. His body was completely broken. It took what breath we had away.

Craig sent out additional emails requesting prayer for the upcoming surgery. He included updates of our son's injuries. My husband expressed our gratefulness for all prayers and concern sent on our son's behalf through emails and phone calls.

We had seen God do so many miracles already. We had no reason to doubt, but we were desperate that He would do more.

We encouraged each other with words from the apostle Paul in Philippians 4:6-7.

Do not be anxious about anything, but in everything, by prayer and petition, with thanksgiving, present your requests to God. And the peace of God, which transcends all understanding, will guard your hearts and our minds in Christ Jesus.

Supernatural peace was necessary to guard my mind as it conjured up images too horrible to let me rest. I pleaded for and received His peace that held together the torn pieces of my mother's heart while I waited.

Hope mixed with sorrow marked our Friday much the same as the two previous heart-wrenching days. In stillness we waited on God to move on our son's behalf, as we experienced a mixture of fragile emotions and a peaceful calmness. We received the much- anticipated update on Bryan's progress from the surgeon around 1:00 p.m. Colorado time. There was a four-hour time difference in Germany. The doctor spoke with confidence about Bryan's condition. He cautioned us about our son's many medical issues and informed us that the orthopedic doctor had adjusted the fixations on his legs while in surgery.

During this phone consult the doctor gave us only a 25% chance of keeping Bryan's right foot. He briefly touched on the painful possibility of a below the knee amputation. Continuing down his checklist he informed us that Bryan's abdominal cavity would remain open. They would not attempt to close it for an additional 4-5 days because of increased swelling. We were told they were able to insert a feeding tube. He would need lots of calories for the healing progress. The plastic surgeon was able to work on our son's facial lacerations and was pleased with the outcome. It had been decided to leave the chest tubes in for now. If Bryan's oxygen levels fell further, he would not be able to fly back home to the United States. It was possible that they might remove them during the next day's scheduled surgery.

At the end of the lengthy conversation, Dr. Sutherlin gave us a 75% chance that our son would be ready to fly home on Sunday. Hope soared that we might be able to see our son soon! We laid down to rest that Friday night covered by a blanket of supernatural peace. Grace stilled us, and Hope tucked us in.

Chapter 8
THE HIDDEN WOUND

A few hours into the night, our fragile rest was interrupted by the shrill sound of the telephone. It was 4:30 a.m. Saturday, March 4. I'm quite certain there is no other way to break devastating information to parents about their child except to just speak it out. Presenting the facts, Bryan's surgeon bluntly told us our son did not have much, if any, brain activity. In the quietness of listening to that single sentence, our grip on hope started to slip. We were stunned by the blow of spoken devastation. This was by far the worst news possible! I was overwhelmed with suppressed sorrow that had to wait for full release.

Dr. Sutherlin methodically explained the new findings. The previous days had been consumed by efforts to keep our son alive as they attended to the obvious wounds that ravished his body. It was only now after Bryan's other grievous injuries had been addressed that their attention had focused on his head injury. The horrible hidden wound of traumatic brain injury was now front and center. Bryan's brain had suffered a complete lack of critical oxygen called anoxia. Brain cells that are deprived of oxygen begin to die after four minutes. In the IED attack Bryan had not been breathing for an undisclosed period. The attempt to intubate him in the battlefield had failed. His brain had also suffered additional critical low oxygen amounts called hypoxia over the course of the ensuing four days. Just *hours* before, he had *again* suffered a lack of oxygen when he was taken down to get the MRI. They had taken him off the bedside oxygen and switched to a less cumbersome hand-held oxygen supply for the trip to radiology. Astonishingly there had been a failure in the placement of the equipment again! His diagnosis was cerebral anoxia, a traumatic brain injury (TBI).

It was a devastating prognosis. We were briefly educated about the Glasgow coma scale of rating severe TBIs. A score of 3 being the worst to 15 being the best. The rating would normally be taken within the first 24 hours after the TBI was incurred. Bryan's initial injury was almost 5 days ago. The doctor said our son currently had a score of 4. He was in a minimally conscious state one point above a vegetative state.

The survival rate after a TBI severe enough to cause a deep coma and low Glasgow score like Bryan's had a very high mortality rate between 76% and 89%. It was doubtful that he would survive. If he did live, the Doctor said it would be in a vegetative state. He suggested we make every effort to get to Germany as soon as possible.

Visions of what the prognosis looked like in my mind's eye threatened to be my undoing as I recalled my son's directive. He did not want to be kept alive in a vegetative state. The torn pieces of my heart were shattered into the smallest of shards. The tears fell unceasingly. With each day the list of injuries had increased. Would these gut-wrenching blows ever stop? How could this be happening? I was incredulous and puzzled. Could it be that to get the news of all his injuries at once would have been beyond our ability to withstand — and then for him to continue to receive additional injury while in the hospital? Only God knows. Perhaps getting the terrible news piece by piece allowed us to better process the stunning sorrow and shattered body of our beloved son. I hadn't imagined that it could get worse. Yet it had.

I cried out for strength and begged for grace. Together we cried out with many tears for our God to intervene and heal our son. We had to believe He was working on our son's behalf. He was our only hope.

Chapter 9
A SUPERNATURAL TOUCH

Plans had already been under way to get Craig and me to Bethesda, Maryland, on Sunday. One additional family member would be allowed to go with us. The plan had been to be at the hospital when Bryan came in from Germany. With the additional information of his expected passing, everything was fluid and changing moment by moment.

We would need a valid passport to fly to Germany. As I searched the safe for our passports, I was dismayed to find that our passports had expired just a few days before. Making the necessary calls we found out that it would take an additional two days to get expedited passports, plus a day to fly from Grand Junction to Delaware. There we would board a flight to Landstuhl, Germany. That flight would take an additional day. The earliest we could be at Bryan's bedside was late Thursday, March 8. Considering the doctor's grave concern for Bryan's passing, that was not soon enough.

We concluded that the expired passports were an affirmation that we should not go to Germany. We decided to bring our son home. Once home, we reasoned, it would give our immediate family the best chance they would have to see him for what could be the final time. I requested that the Marine Corps do whatever was humanly possible to make sure Bryan was on Sunday's flight back to the United States. The sum of my mother's heart wanted him home. If I had to say goodbye to my son, I wanted it to be on American soil. I didn't want his passing to be on foreign soil.

"Oh, my Father!" I cried. "Please bring my warrior child home! Have mercy on us dear Lord Jesus! Please heal our child!" This was the cry of my heart.

The news we had just received was so staggering it was physically debilitating. We were thankful for the tangible presence of the Comforter through the prayers of the body of Christ. We yearned for the presence of family. We had a deep-seated need to gather our daughters around us. No one else loved him as deeply as his sisters. Jennifer was not far away and could come quickly. Hollie Mae was still in Grand Junction. We were desperate to formulate a plan that included their input, yet we couldn't imagine rousing them from sleep to deliver such staggering news.

We waited for the sun to break the eastern skyline before asking a close friend of Hollie's to go awaken her and bring her to us. There was no easy way to tell Jennifer and Hollie about their brother's current prognosis. We were rightly stunned by the crushing blow.

Craig immediately reached out by email to those praying for Bryan. Again, he urgently requested intercession for our son. He informed our praying friends that we were in an overwhelming crisis that involved a period of waiting. Bryan needed the Divine Healer to increase his brain activity. If there was ANY increase, the doctor would consider moving him back to the states. Lack of movement ensured the trip home aboard the air force's flying ICU would never happen. Without intervention of a supernatural touch from the hand of our loving Creator, we knew Bryan's brief stay on this side of eternity would soon be over.

We valued the prayers of the saints more than our next labored breath. The Holy Spirit took those very labored prayers and multiplied them across the world.

As we waited for our daughters to arrive, we prayed for the presence of the Spirit to enable us to share the heartbreaking diagnosis from the neurosurgeon. How do you tell those most dear to you the crushing news of their beloved brother's likely passing? It felt so bluntly cruel when the doctor told us to expect no more than a vegetative state. How do you share that? The day passed under an ominous battle cloud of grief as we warred despair that threatened to overtake our settled hope in the heavenlies. Close friends came to bring comfort by helping with the children and preparing them a meal to eat. The little ones were blessed in their innocence and played normally at our feet. I struggled with fear and grief for my son. Peace eluded us as we were face-first in tearful, desperate prayers of lament for our son. Gratefully the eternal day of waiting was finally over.

Bryan showed trace signs of random movement in his extremities. These small movements secured him a ride home in the Air Force Flying ICU. Our one and only son was bundled into his flight at 3:00 a.m. on a dark Sunday morning.

How fitting that he should be coming home on a Sunday. It was a Sunday when the recruiter came and took him from us all those long days ago. The date was Sunday, March 4, 2007. At long last our son was on his way back home.

Chapter 10
JOURNEY
TO THE UNKNOWN

In the early morning hours, we received our government's invitation to fly to Bryan's bedside. Arrangements for flights and lodging would be secured for us. In those dark hours teetering on the edge of despair, I contemplated the future.

The smallest of decisions provoked deep labored thought as I attempted to set my house and life in order. I couldn't imagine the future with the script we had been given. I was devastated beyond anything I could have even imagined. I knew the Holy Spirit would have to do the living through me. I was a child again. I needed to be told what to do. I knew Bryan's life had changed forever. I painfully considered that he might not be coming back home to this house . I also acknowledged that each of our lives had been altered dramatically. Would God answer our prayers for our son to be healed physically? Again, I had no doubt that He had the power to do so. Would He? How long would we be in this alternate universe called Washington, D.C.?

I knew I would stay as long as it took given the chance. Oh, how I begged for the chance!! I cried out in the dark for strength to live out in the light of future days what I was being called to do. I was being offered a chance to trust in my sovereign God.

My thoughts wandered. Would Craig be able to stay with me? His business would not survive without him. I was not sure I would survive without him. He was so strong in his faith. He too had been through dark times and found God to meet him there with hope and healing. Other random thoughts entered my troubled mind. Who would take care of the dog and cat? What about the ladies Bible study I led at my home? I prayed my friends would continue meeting somewhere. Other thoughts came to me. Who would love on those grandchildren I adored? Hollie would go with us, but what about my other daughter Jennifer? How could I leave her behind? She would need help with those short ones, for sure.

All these unanswered questions threatened to overwhelm me. I had one final question as the pressing and practical need to prepare set in. How does one pack for a trip to the unknown?

After a lifetime of moments that seem to pass in slow motion, I stuffed a mismatched collection of casual "Colorado meets Washington, D.C." apparel into a small carry-on and called it done.

The early morning trip to the airport was silent except for muffled sounds of sorrow mingled with K LOVE on the radio. At one point during the hour-long journey, I voiced the very real possibility of having to say goodbye to Bryan. Hollie hotly contested even the thought of it! She said her brother was a necessary part of the abundant life God had promised her. I assured her that my hope was in God healing Bryan. She made me promise I had not given up believing that God could do miracles. I made a mental note that perhaps I should keep my anguished thoughts to myself.

Craig, Hollie and I boarded the plane at the small regional airport in Grand Junction. As we settled in for the long day of travel ahead, I sensed the presence of another passenger traveling with us. He was seen only with eyes of faith. I was so thankful I could see Him. I could never have made the trip without Him.

As the plane soared to cruising altitude, I sat still in my seat with no more chores to be done, no more arrangements to be made. I felt the weight of all that had transpired in the last four days upon my heart and mind. I wished I could store the excess burdens I carried like one stows baggage in the overhead compartment. I attempted to maintain control over my emotions but lost the battle straightway. Fumbling in my bag, I dug out my Bible to reconcile my tormented feelings with all that I knew to be true of God and His Word.

As I examined my feelings, I was surprised by the quietness that settled in my spirit. Unexpected relief flowed over me. I had physically done all I could do. The wait was over. I was trusting God to take me to my son. I collapsed into His presence and mentally handed Him my numbered *to do* list along with the extra unseen baggage I carried on with me. He personally stowed the excess in the overhead and took note of the list I surrendered. Tops on the list I gave Him was… maintain composure. I sat before him and wept. Then I wept and wept some more. Never had I been so broken.

The Short Ones

Chapter 11

FLASHBACK

As the day of air travel progressed, I wondered how I could continue to have so many tears? Would they ever run dry? How could I find comfort in familiar pages of scripture if I couldn't see through this river of sorrow that flowed freely down my face, neck and soaked the front of my blouse? Grateful for the roar of the engine, I cried out in muffled sobs to my Father God for His help in this time of great need and distress.

I heard the Word whisper to my soul, *remember*. Suddenly the current of tears slowed to a gentler stream as I recognized His voice in my inner being. Yes! Yes, I would remember! There was much to remember!

The interior cabin of the plane and those around me fled away. Immediately I was transported in my memory to the time I first heard of this God in whom I had grown to have so much trust.

It was Christmas Day. I was a six-year-old child. My siblings and I awoke to a house full of emptiness. In previous days the same furniture company that had delivered all the beautiful furniture only a few short weeks before had come and taken everything away. Everything. Our towering bunk beds with the ladders were gone. The bed linens lay in various piles in the corner of empty rooms. Our beautiful teal green sofa, the one with expansive, brushable leather that I had delighted to trace childish figures upon, was gone. So was the desk I felt sure was mine alone. Our kitchen table was gone. Our refrigerator was gone. Everything was gone.

The only things left were not *things* at all, but people — a young mother, a new baby sister, and four children ranging in ages 6 to 12. We had been transplanted by our earthly father from our homeland of the great state of Texas to South Sioux City, Nebraska, just months prior. Then he had walked out of our lives. He had abandoned us there. The empty house was proof that we could no longer pretend to be a normal family. We had never been normal. Our father never stayed long. That Christmas morning my mother gave each of us a small wrapped gift. We opened it to find a small book. It was a Gideon Bible. She shared with us that this book was indeed very, very special. It was written by God. She told us that God had a son named Jesus who was born on Christmas day. Mother said that God loved Jesus very much. Christmas was a celebration of the birth of baby Jesus. It wasn't about Santa Claus and presents under a tree.

As a six-year-old I was amazed at this! I considered my mother's tear stained face and heard her softly trembling voice. I accepted her words and gift with great wonder. I was particularly enamored with the God who had a baby boy that he loved very much. I wondered what it would be like to have a father who loved me very much?

As memories piled upon memories, I remembered the day I cried out to this Father of Jesus Christ. I had hidden my seven- year-old self in a small dilapidated shed on the same worn-down rental property where we had been cast aside. That particularly horrid day, I had come to the end of myself. I hated the awfulness of what went on in that house. I raged at the family I had, at the secrets I was forced to keep. I reasoned if I had a father like Jesus did — one who loved me — I wouldn't be left to defend myself from such ugly despair.

Having audibly spent rage bigger than my stature, my sobs became hiccups and I grew silent.

"Ask me."

It was more of an intense inner voice than an audible voice.

"Ask me to be your Father."

Huddled in that corner I was amazed that I had just heard God offer to be my Father! Right there, trembling in the presence of weighty otherness, I cried out and asked the Father of Jesus Christ to be my Father too. He said yes.

The circumstances of my life didn't change that day. The truth is many years passed. Fear and sorrow increased. But that day I changed. I now had a Father that I could talk to. I would return often to my hiding place and pour out my heart in lament to my new Father.

Now as we raced above the clouds on that plane, I recounted the faithfulness of that very same God throughout my life. I drew strength from a lifetime of promises found in His word and the supporting memories I guarded like treasure. Soon my spirit within me was emboldened. Whatever the future held I would not face it alone. My Father would be with me and, His Word would be my compass.

No, my belief in the Bible was not just intellectual nor did I think it was just some dusty old book of ideals reserved for Sundays. It was special just like my Mother told me all those years ago. The Word was God-breathed and became my daily habit. I thirsted for it. I could never get enough. Truth and hope were waiting to be uncovered there. Once found, hope believed and lived out, however painful, would keep my eyes fixed on the eternal in what would be a long journey into the unknown. Of this I was certain.

Chapter 12

THE WAIT

We arrived in Washington, D.C., in the early evening hours Sunday, March 4. The Marine Corps sent a van to pick us up and take us to the famed National Naval Medical Center in Bethesda, Maryland.

Looking out the window of the van as we sped along the George Washington Memorial Parkway, I gazed upon the Potomac River. Memories of family vacations taken here in our nation's capital flashed across the movie screen of my mind. Our children had been much younger. We had visited many of the monuments now recognizable along the way. Never would I have imagined that we would be coming back here under these grim circumstances.

Tears gathered in my eyes as I longed to have a do-over. If I could just go back in time to revisit those days, I would tightly gather a much younger little boy in my arms and delight in his childish exuberance.

Upon arrival we were escorted into the flag-lined front entrance of the historic President's hospital and down a side hall to the Marine Corps Liaison Office. It had been an exhausting day of travel and yet our overwhelming desire to see our son gave us motivation, so our weariness in part vanished. Every step of the way there was protocol to adhere to. We quickly came to understand that nothing was going to happen fast despite the urgency of which we had been instructed to come to our son's bedside.

After attending to the request of signatures on multiple documents presented to us by our government, we were invited into the outer room to wait. As time crawled by, we were pleased to meet so many military personnel. There were corporals, sergeants, staff sergeants, gunnery sergeants and even a master sergeant, but the one we desperately wanted to meet again was a precious Lance Corporal. We called him Son. As the clock slowly inched closer to midnight we were finally escorted up to the ICU where we were assured that we would see our son. We were ushered into a conference room where we were to wait for the attending doctor. Once there, we continued to be stalled. They simply were not ready for us to see our son! Why? My heart pounded within me. Had something gone wrong? Couldn't they comprehend how great our need was to see him face to face before it was too late?

The doctor in Germany urged us to get to our son's bedside as soon as possible. Surely, they could guess the anxiety in our hearts. It had been seven very long months since those last moments of leave in August. Tears welled up in my eyes and spilled over as I clutched my worn Bible close to my heart. We had been in the hospital for over three hours and I was seriously contemplating going on a room to room search for my son. Silently I cried out for God's presence to fill us with His peace and patience as we continued to wait. As we quietly talked to one another, a slender woman slipped into the conference room and introduced herself as one of the doctors attending Bryan.

Anticipation built as I sprang to my feet eager to follow her to Bryan's bedside. Slowly and with studied precision, she pulled out a chair and sat down. She proceeded to calmly ask each of us about our relationship to Bryan. As she studied my face, I studied hers. She looked to be in her early thirties. She may have been much younger but no doubt her career choice had taken a toll on her facial features. I sensed her guarded eyes and professionalism as she looked past me to my husband. I could tell those eyes had seen much in this place of sorrowful hope.

Slowly I again took a seat. I saw in those moments a person who was covertly discerning my potential reaction as a mom of a gravely injured child. She had been chosen to be the one to take me back to see my son. She was unsure of my response. She probably thought I would faint when I saw our son's fragile state. I felt compassion for her quandary. She pressed us to ask questions.

I knew what she meant. She wanted me to ask medical questions. Ones that she could answer. She didn't have the answers to the questions I had. Only God had those answers. Would my son live? Would he recover from this devastation of war? Would we cling to our God in spite of the horror ahead? Would I lose my faith? Could I lose my faith? These were the questions I had.

I wanted reassurance and answers that she could not give. I knew that, so I asked the one question that she could answer. When can I see my son? She looked down at the chart she had in front of her and began to recite some of Bryan's grievous injuries.

After a few long moments I interrupted her. I firmly assured her I was well aware of his injuries. I had spent hours that turned into days praying over each one. There would be time to talk over medical issues. Right now, I wanted to see my son. With growing passion, I told her that I was stronger than the person she saw before her. With certainty I assured her I would not faint. I pleaded my case. The time had come to see my son. My heart could wait no longer.

As we left the conference room and followed her down the darkened ICU corridor, she continued to give us instructions in preparation of us seeing our dear son.

Chapter 13
THROUGH
A MOTHER'S EYES

If you would question each of us separately about our memory of those first few sacred moments when our eyes beheld Bryan for the first time, you would find we each remember those moments differently. I recall the room where he lay as being dimly lit. "No, Mom!" Hollie would exclaim. "There were bright lights on everywhere! The doctor had just finished inserting the probe into his head! Remember?"

No. I had tunnel vision. I saw his precious face through the eyes of a mother. I paused at the door for a moment in time and proclaimed incredibly, "He's Beautiful! Look at him!" I exclaimed in wonder. "When did he grow from being a boy into a man? He's so big! He's so beautiful!"

His large tall six-feet two-inch, 220-pound muscular frame consumed the bed he lay in. I spoke to no one and yet to everyone present. "He's all there!" I proclaimed in amazement.

I saw toes I hadn't expected to see as I quickly searched his right leg with my eyes. "Bryan is ALL there!" I repeated in wonder as I went to his bedside.

"Hi Bryan." I whispered as I caressed his face and kissed his forehead. "It's Mom. I'm here! God brought you home to us!" I said, rejoicing. "You're home! You are back in the USA! I love you so much, Bryan."

I quickly knelt by his bedside, rejecting the urge to wait and do in private what I knew I needed to do immediately. I praised God for bringing my son home. I thanked Him for sparing his life and for allowing us to see him again. In those sacred moments, Bryan's bed became an altar of sacrifice. It was a holy place where I surrendered my only son to the will of God. Then I got up, took inventory of his grievous wounds, and asked with fresh faith that Jehovah Rapha, the God who heals, would mend each one. Much the way a mother searches the body of her newborn child, I searched the body of my warrior child. I did not turn away from one injury that I could see. I marveled at toes I had not expected to see. I bent down and kissed them. I searched his face that had been torn and traced each stitch with my eyes. I saw spent emotion in closed eyes as moisture trickled sideways into stubble missed by the razor's edge. I witnessed the dried blood that had run down his temples and into his ears. My eyes observed that the Iraqi sand caked in his hair took on a reddish tone when mixed with his life's blood. His haircut was high and tight (emphasis on high). I smiled. The remaining two inches on top stood straight up. It was filthy yet comical. I wondered why it had not been washed.

I lifted the sheet they had draped across his body. His abdomen was greatly distended, and he was open from the middle of his chest to his nether regions. He was filled with surgical packing that was secured by an incredibly large clear bandage stained golden yellow by the betadine they had used to wash out his wounds. It reminded me of a huge clear carpet runner. There were large tubes coming out of both sides of his chest. There were tubes everywhere. My mind registered the mini pump they had secured to his left leg. His right leg was completely encased in bandages with only his toes sticking out. I gently took each hand into mine individually and searched each one carefully. They were intact but peppered with small wounds. Even though he had been pulled out of smoldering wreckage, he had only one quarter-sized burn on his right hand. I marveled through misty eyes, completely humbled. Gently I laid the sheet back across his body.

Too soon we were asked to leave his side as buzzers and alerts started going off in response to increased heart rate and climbing blood pressure. Exchanging names and phone numbers in the event we were urgently needed, we were rushed from the room as a number of medical personnel quickly entered.

It was well after midnight as we, fueled by adrenaline, fairly walked/ran on air through the cold night. We searched our way through the nearby streets to find our place of lodging. It never occurred to us to ask for a ride.

Chapter 14

BROKEN

It was a lengthy walk from our temporary lodging to the grounds of The National Naval Medical Center. My senses were immediately convinced that we were indeed in a different world. Flashy cars of all makes and models flew by on the narrow street as the city awoke to meet the cold crisp morning of a new day. As dawn was breaking, bright lights shone still from commercial high-rise buildings, apartments, businesses and private residences. A high fence surrounded the Naval hospital. We walked toward an opening in the fence. It was obvious that it wasn't a pedestrian entrance, but we took our place among the cars in line and waited our turn.

Arriving at the guard shack we were asked to produce ID and questioned as to why we were there. After verifying that Lance Corporal Bryan Chambers was indeed a patient and presenting our orders, we were allowed to continue on our way to an entrance into the hospital. Once inside, the hospital was a vast maze of passageways going in every direction. Unlike the night before, the hallways were overflowing with uniformed military personnel and medical staff each on a mission of purpose.

We joined the overwhelming current of people and searched signs to find our way to our son's bedside. Our hearts were greatly encouraged to see that our son was more responsive than he had been the night before. Incredibly Bryan was smiling around his breathing tube and opening his eyes on command! When we asked him to squeeze our fingers — he did just that! We recognized it for the miracle it was!

The doctor in Germany told us that Bryan likely would not live. He said if he survived, we would have to live with a very impaired son. Clearly God was healing our son! We were quick and very vocal to give Him praise.

We were again very quickly informed that, because of a critical lack of oxygen on the field and in Germany, there had been severe brain damage. His team of doctors had put a brain bolt in the high portion of his forehead. Though it certainly looked very disturbing, it was necessary to monitor the oxygen to his brain and alert them to the possible dangerous buildup of pressure.

The brain injury was manifesting in the same way as a stroke victim. He had much less response on his left side, particularly his left arm and hand. The neurosurgeon told us that the brain damage was non-reversible. We immediately started praying and believing that God would intervene and restore full use of his entire left side and heal his brain.

The next injury addressed was his legs. Both legs currently had little sensation to pain and appeared to be paralyzed. The ortho doctor informed us that Bryan's right leg had been very damaged, but that he was encouraged to see the wound high on his upper leg improving. The medical team was formulating a plan to put a rod alongside his femur to assist with its healing. His tibia and fibula had shown some improvement, and the surface wounds were healing. His right foot was significantly damaged. His heel was gone. There was no connecting bone left between his ankle and his foot. That bone was crucial and there was little they could do to replace it. The doctor began to talk to us about the positive results that could be achieved with the use of a prosthetic in the event that he regained feeling in his legs.

The breathing tube that had been in his mouth had been removed and replaced with a trache in his throat after he had returned from that day's surgery.

We were pleased to have that removed so that he could smile. His nurse lifted our spirits with a story she told of her interaction with Bryan. She had come in earlier to wake him up. As she told him he was back in the USA, he presented her with the biggest grin she had ever seen with a breathing tube!

Sure enough, as Craig played Chris Tomlin's *Everlasting God* for Bryan, his eyes got wide. A smile split across his face. Hope and faith soared in our hearts!

Within minutes there were more doctors to meet. We were told that he had additional fractures that needed healing. He had a broken jaw. His pelvis was broken. With each uncovered wound I felt a deeper sorrow in my mother's heart. Very concerning to them was the massive bruise high on his hip and buttocks continuing up his back.

There appeared to be massive muscle damage. The muscle had detached from the pelvic bone and possibly from his spinal cord. I held on to the bed's railing as my knees suddenly threatened to buckle beneath me, but just as suddenly I felt God to be my strength.

They would take him back to surgery to assess the injury and re-attach the muscle. While he was in surgery, they would also call in the plastic surgeon.

The next medical team we met was his urologist and associates. Bryan's right kidney had been severely injured. They would be monitoring it closely and take action should complications arise. The doctor explained to us that as a result of the blast our son had lost his right testicle. His remaining testicle was very bruised and had required surgery in the field where all foreign materials that might promote infection and impede healing were removed. He was hopeful that blood flow would continue and with time it would heal.

We were desperate in conveying our desire that they would consider this issue a high priority. We knew Bryan would desire children one day and our hearts broke at the thought of him losing that privilege. I was overwhelmed by this latest sacrifice my son and our family might have to endure.

"No, Lord!" I pleaded. "Please, no. Please, not this?! Please, we need children!" Once again, I breathed a not so silent prayer that this sorrow would pass us by.

Our next consult was with the Infectious Disease team. We were informed that everyone that comes from serving in Iraq has some odd skin bacteria that lives in the soil there. As a common rule, this creates no complications for healthy individuals, but for Bryan it would be dangerous as the bacteria entered his body through his many open wounds. The treatment was going to have to be very aggressive as the bacteria had already begun to spread and colonize throughout his body. We would be required to *suit up* with a gown, gloves and mask upon entering his room. Direct skin to skin contact was discouraged.

As night crept into the spent day, so the pain Bryan was experiencing replaced the smiles with anguish and tears. As we anxiously tried to comfort our son, the doctor ordered an ultrasound. He gave us the grim news that in the morning there was a very real possibility that they were going to have to remove Bryan's last testicle when they took him back for surgery. My heart was torn anew. Just hours earlier we had been reassured that it was healing. Now it was life threatening. We were freshly devastated. The doctors told us that the tissue had likely been dead for a while. At 11:00 p.m. we were required to leave till visiting hours resumed at 8:00 a.m. in the morning.

It was incredibly hard to leave our suffering son. I couldn't hold back the tears that came like a flash flood. I had only been reunited with him for one day.

"Please, Father, I need more time." I whispered.

Walking back to our hotel we had reason to cry out to God with grateful hearts. We had witnessed so much, it was hard to process. Our hearts were also heavy. Bryan was so injured!

Together we cried out with faces to the floor for God's intervention once again. Despite all the injuries we witnessed in our son's body, we had walked back with the gift of faith to believe that our son was not going to die this day. We had seen our God answer a specific prayer. Bryan was alive!

Chapter 15

TOGETHER WE CRIED

That first day proved to be a pattern of many marathon days to follow. Always, there was much for which to praise God and to plead for in the throne room of grace. The intense battle to save Bryan's life was like riding a never-ending emotional roller coaster with unexpected twists and turns that leave one nauseated and disoriented. The depth of pain and suffering our precious son displayed compelled us to stay on our knees in the presence of God.

We found no time or space in private to make our request known to the Father, so we very publicly made his room and the waiting room our altars of prayer and filled it with songs of worship and pleas of deliverance. Our audible cries of brokenness and need drove us into the presence of the God who invited us to bring all that concerned us to Him. We humbled ourselves and together we cried out for Bryan's healing. We continued to plead through word of mouth and e-mail for fellow believers to lift him up in prayer.

March 7, 2007

Dear Family and Friends,

It has been another long day here in Bethesda. We are always praising God for His mercies which are new every morning! We have more news and prayer requests to make.

Bryan was very responsive this morning. He was smiling so much the nurses gave him another point-he is at an eleven! We are excited about this and are continuing to pray that the numbers stay high and continue to rise.

Late last night after I had sent out the last update the doctors told Mom and Dad that after another ultrasound that they were going to have to remove

Bryan's last testicle. This was devastating to everyone. We had prayed that God would heal this and since we had not heard anything new, we had assumed it was a non-issue. So last night all the fears were brought back up. The doctors told Mom and Dad that the tissue had been dead for a while. The pain Bryan was feeling, they told us, was due to the testicle issue. We hit the floor asking God for one more miracle.

Most of the day Bryan was in surgery. He was the first one in from the ICU due to the severity of pain that he was in. When the urologist came to see us midway through the surgery, he told us there was blood flow to the testicle and though the surgeons had to take a portion of it, there IS enough for testosterone and a high possibility for babies!!! Praise God! What the doctors had seen was a blood clot that was blocking the view of the testicle- God knew all along, He is so faithful.

We continue to praise the God who gives and takes away — Bryan had to have his right foot taken off this morning. This was very, very, hard for us and will be tough for Bryan also- so please keep praying. The foot had gotten worse and was making the rest of his body weak, it clearly had to go but it is sad to see. We KNOW God is good and we are praising Him through this storm.

The infection is still causing Bryan to have a temperature that is very high. The doctors have him outfitted with a special suit to regulate his temperature, keep him warm when he needs it and cool when he gets hot. The doctors are pushing very powerful meds through him to fight off this infection. Please keep praying! Here is the address that anyone can send letters or notes to Bryan.

We love you all and are so grateful for your prayers. I know that we keep saying this, but it remains true — we are confident that aside from prayer Bryan wouldn't be here. God does miracles so great and your prayers have been and continue to be such a huge part of this.

March 8, 2007

Dear Family and Friends,

It has been such an encouragement to hear from you these past couple of days. Your notes of concern and your prayers have been such a blessing to all of us. We are blessed to have so many people that love and care for Bryan praying. We BELIEVE in prayer and every day as we see the effects of our combined prayers, we believe Him a little bit more.

The doctors have Bryan on a morphine drip and that seems to be helping the pain some. They plan to close his stomach up tomorrow after one last wash out. He does have that nasty bug from Iraq and the doctors have mixed a combo of meds to strategically fight it off. Please be praying that the meds would work effectively and that we would soon be able to touch Bryan skin to skin without the gown, gloves, and mask. The urologist reports that everything (down there) is healing very well and that they are pleased. Bryan is still on the trachea tube and he is still battling a high temperature that makes him uncomfortable — keep praying for those issues. All in all, we have a miraculous Creator, one who knows Bryan's body incredibly well and He is patching and mending Bryan one day at a time. Praise Him!

It is going to be a marathon for Mom and Dad.

Mom is feeling a little bit better and last night she got eight hours of sleep! Keep her in your prayers, for strength and for good health. Dad has been able to clear off his work schedule. Isaiah will be picking up the slack, and Dad plans to stay here with Mom for the rest of the month. Jen and Isaiah had to head back to Colorado today and it was hard to see them go. We are thankful that God orchestrated this family reunion here in D.C. — it was so good to be together again, even if only briefly.

Grandma and Grandpa Chambers as well as Aunt Cindy, Uncle Curt and Aunt Colleen arrived in the afternoon today. They report that Bryan is looking much better than they expected (we're a little biased but we think so too)! Hollie is doing fine, holding up alright.

She donated blood today at the hospital (maybe not the smartest of ideas) — she and Bryan have type O blood and they are going to mark the blood to go to Bryan if it's needed.

Thank you everyone for your concern and prayers, we have been overwhelmed by your love and prayers- there is no way we could ever repay you or thank-you enough. God is good all the time and we know that part of His goodness to us has been all of you. Be encouraged- Bryan is healing and we are praising God!

Praise be to the Lord, for he has heard my cry for mercy. The Lord is my strength and my shield; my heart trust in hi, and I am helped. My heart leaps for joy and I will give thanks to him in song.

The Lord is the strength of his people, a fortress of salvation for his anointed one. Save your people and bless your inheritance; be their shepherd and carry them forever. Psalms 28:6-9

We love you so much-be blessed and take good care of yourself!

Love and Thanks,
The Chambers Family

On the 10th of March Craig sent out the following email. The latest from Bethesda Naval Medical,

Hey y'all, I am giving my precious brown-eyed girl the night off. She has done an amazing job keeping all of you updated. Informed prayer warriors, I believe, are more effective than the uninformed. Kudos' to my Hollie Mae.

As always, I want to begin with much loud and long praise to the God who gives and takes away. As we know, if we believed in a God who only gives and never had the power to take away, somehow, He wouldn't quite be God, now would He? We totally rest in His mercy and grace which actually shows up around here every day, totally regardless of the fact that we do not deserve it. Yet every day when we arise there it is again.

In many ways today was a more quiet day for our hero. Another day back to the operating room, but that somehow is nearly normal around here. The surgeons closed almost all of his abdominal wounds, only leaving a small area down low open.

The plastic surgeons took out all of Bryan's stitches in his face and around his mouth and eye. The surgeons washed out all his wounds and flushed them again attempting to totally remove all sources of possible infection. The urologist gave him a clean bill of health and removed all stitches and tubes down there.

We had above-the-top care today as he had two nurses attending him, which was a blessing. Bryan even got a haircut today and of course they gave him a perfect high and tight, befitting to the Marine Corp. regs.

Top 3 current prayer needs:
1 – White blood cell count needs to come down
2 – His awake time and alertness needs to improve
3 – The pain management (or lack thereof) is always a juggling act. The side effects for Bryan are high blood pressure, increased heart rate, and high fevers.

As I type this at midnight, we have been moved to the Fisher House, which is super nice and a huge blessing to us. Kind of like a Ronald McDonald house, only on steroids. The days are incredibly long here and come with its own version of mental and psychological stress that is almost impossible to imagine if you have never been in a similar situation. I have been totally amazed, beyond words, by the ability for us to go on, purely by the power of your prayers. So please keep them coming — they are more highly valued by us that you will never know.

My beloved Granda Lea, special partner of nearly twenty-nine years is really battling some physical ailments and some super sleep and fatigue issues. Please pray for health and well-being during this long and trying time. The surgeon gave us the best word picture that we have heard. Picture this time in Bryan's life as a long-distance marathon and his first week is but ten feet into it.

One of the absolute highlights of our day is the time we get to sit down and read all of the many emails that you have all sent to us. They truly lift us up on eagle's wings and make our spirits soar. Every hurting person in this hospital is vitally counting on prayer. We happen to believe that this battle we are in, is as much spiritual as it is physical. Consequently, prayer is the key to winning this battle.

The verse that Hollie and I keep coming back to is (I think from Psalms 27). "I am still confident of this: I will see the goodness of the Lord in the land of the living." The goodness of the Lord washes over us every day in waves. We only have to look to Bryan's left and to his right to see young men in much worse condition than he is. Bottom line: we believe that our God is good all of the time, and we will, by faith, praise Him in this storm. Thanks to the technology of ipods, Bryan goes to bed every night and wakes every morning to the words of the song

"Everlasting God" ringing in his ears (Chris Tomlin's See the Morning CD). Invariably when we play it for him, he wakes up and his eyes tell us he is indeed hearing it.

Thanks-again for being such a huge part of all these miracles that our Everlasting God is doing for this family here in this naval hospital.

Love and hugs to y'all,
Craig, Granda, Hollie and Jennifer

Another email went out around the globe on March 11th.

Dear, dear friends, family and MIGHTY prayer warriors,

It has been a long day here at the naval hospital. We are grateful to our Father who is providing us with enough strength, courage, and mercy for every day. It has not been easy, but God has been good. We remain grateful that you continue to pray with us and for us. It has been so humbling and encouraging to know that prayers are carrying us. We could never hope to walk this journey alone in our own strength with only our own prayers. — THANK YOU!!

Bryan is hanging in there like the tough Marine he is. There have been little changes to report. He is still battling the high white blood cell count due to the infection. The doctors are pumping him full of medicine, but it is just a process that takes time. Bryan has also developed pneumonia in both of his lungs. The nurses have been trying to clear out some of the gunk that develops in his lungs that he can't cough out because of his injuries. This, along with some breathing treatments, will help clear this up but it too will take time. Additionally, Bryan has developed a bad bed sore on the back of his head because of pressure and swelling of his head through the donut pillow against the bed. Please pray for all these issues. They are important and God doesn't overlook anything. We remember He is into the smallest of details as well as the big stuff.

We would love to see Bryan more active. During the first few days he was responding quite a bit: smiling, squeezing our fingers, and blinking. These past couple days there has been little response. We KNOW Bryan is in there and we KNOW that God can call light out of darkness. We are praying that Bryan would have peace and hope circulating in his mind, and that while he is "sleeping" God would be speaking to him and encouraging him. There is the hope that as the medication continues to wear off from all the surgeries that he has endured these past days that his responses would become stronger. Bryan may very well be sensitive to the meds and this could be part of the reason for the stillness. Right now, it may be that he needs the sleep and the rest, and that full consciousness would be too traumatic for him. We are trying to pray for what is best for BRYAN not just for us- this is easier said than done!

God orchestrated several incredibly sweet and beautiful meetings for us today. One of those was meeting Bryan's former Lieutenant Andrew, who had been with Bryan in

Iraq. He had been the one who stepped on an IED after telling Bryan to stay and work on his vehicle. His injures sent him to Bethesda were he literally spent months in the ICU unit where Bryan is now. Andrew is a double amputee well above his knees. His testimony and witness in such devastation is affecting lives. He had a lot of good advice having been on the other side of the bed. It was kind of him to come meet with us and to check on Bryan. God has appeared to remove any bitterness from Andrew's life regarding the attack and we are praying that God will do the same for Bryan. Also, there was a very kind Marine mother of one of the crewmen that was in the vehicle with Bryan during the explosion. She connected with us today (yet another God appointment that He made happen). Her son had been with Bryan and helped dig him out of the wreckage. She was very worried about Bryan and was on orders from her son to see if Bryan's family had made it to the hospital. Both meetings show the compassionate heart of our Father who does things for his kids not just because it's necessary but because He delights to!

We are all doing fine. Mom is slowly getting better each day and for that we are thankful. Thanks for praying with us! Emotionally we are battered and hurting, but we know that God is rich in mercy and abounding in love. Please keep praying with us- you will NEVER know how much your prayer is helping us and changing Bryan through God's mighty right arm. We appreciate your notes of encouragement and phone calls. It gladdens our hearts to hear from you all.

PLEASE — understand this: our actions, our faith, and our hope comes from our Father who is carrying us

through this storm. Apart from His intervention and His grace we would not be here, and we would not be able to believe Him. We cannot imagine where we would be if not for His love and His mercy - He is so worthy and deserving of ALL praise. If there is any testimony in our lives these past few days- we know this - it is because of His mercies that we are not consumed. We love you all and appreciate you more than we could say.
With Love, Grace and Praise,
The Chambers Family

The response was supernatural. The Spirit moved in hearts around the world as prayer warriors shared Bryan's story through words of witness and as they forwarded our emails. Numerous churches in Washington, D.C., and throughout the nation responded in faith, believing God could and would heal this young Lance Corporal from his bed of suffering. Visitors and prayer warriors began arriving in numbers. They were believing God to send healing to our young Marine. Nurses and doctors responded to our open display of faith in God. They knew we were praying for our son and for them. They were first-hand witnesses to the healings that defied medical logic.

Our believing faith along with the acting, compassionate faith of untold thousands to pray, was a gift from God that moved the Healer to act. The body of Christ held our arms up high and together we cried for the healing of a young Marine.

In his faithfulness, God did a great work in the lives of many who prayed for him. Together we learned to persevere in prayer using scripture to intercede for Bryan.

Volumes of encouraging emails from people across America and around the world are posted on Bryan's Caringbridge website as a permanent unchanging testimony of their heartfelt concern and love for an American hero. Boxes upon boxes of cards were sent to us through the mail. School children across the USA wrote precious letters and colored drawings of well wishes and love.

It would appear Bryan became the recipient of the outpouring of love and respect for those who would willingly put their lives on the line for their country. He represented the 1% of those willing to serve.

"Bryan could have been my son!" Many proclaimed, "I've NEVER prayed for anyone like I prayed for Bryan! Not even my own children!" I was completely humbled.

We heard these statements many times over. My capacity to love grew for these dear prayer warriors who gave of their time and entered our suffering with us. I was seeing the body of Christ function in a way that I had never seen. They were actively meeting tangible physical needs that we had.

Our dear friend, Dan, a fellow veteran of wars past, busied himself collecting resources in small soup cans he was allowed to place at businesses in our hometown and surrounding communities. A special lady cooked us many a homemade meal to eat in our room. New found friends brought us snacks to eat when we didn't have time to sit down. Still others sent us gifts, took care of our pets, maintained our yard in Colorado and did maintenance on our home in our long absence. Within a few days our ability to keep up with phone calls and email correspondence became impossible.

We were providentially directed to a website where we were able to post updates on Bryan's condition quickly. This proved to be an invaluable resource. It was through this venue God gave my husband Craig an outlet for his desire to minister and give God praise. This site allowed him to journal daily in real time his thoughts and prayer requests. It was perfect.

Our daughter, Hollie Mae, also ministered on the website with great faith and effectiveness. She reached into many lives with her obvious love and concern for her brother.

Our God did miracles in Bryan's life routinely. Thousands were witness to the God we depended on while our son was on his journey back to the land of the living. Soon our name was known in the President's Hospital. We were the family who prayed. Out loud. Anywhere. Everywhere. On our knees.

Not everyone responded positively to the public exercising of our faith. I imagine we created embarrassment for some who did not share our desperate need. The open practice of our Christian faith was not very politically correct in the very political corridors of The National Naval Medical Center. People took notice. The enemy took notice.

It was clear from the beginning days of Bryan's journey into the culture of medical care within the Department of Defense that God had a plan that included his family's presence. He knew that Bryan would need more than one advocate to watch over his life.

All too soon we were consistently shocked to realize that even though Bryan had survived the war in Iraq, he was still very much in a battle of survival stateside. The very medical institution that he had been brought to for healing would become an unexpected battleground. We had entered a struggle that would test our beliefs on a moment by moment basis. There was an unseen spiritual enemy that relentlessly desired to take our son's life. We dared not let our guard down. The experience would leave us battle worn and bruised but stronger in our faith. We clung to the truth of the word of God despite circumstances that propelled us farther beyond our natural abilities to endure. We were in a storm, both spiritual and political.

At times the brewing storm threatened to overtake us as we were swept into its depths. We were stunned at the gale force that struck our family unit and threatened to pull us apart even as we desperately clung to one another. We had little knowledge of the tempest that we had entered in Washington, D.C. The clash of congressional and bureaucratic decisions made in previous months and years would profoundly affect us along with other hurting families that came by the thousands to live long term while their heroes slowly and painfully recovered.

We could not have known that the leaders of our country would implement policies that encouraged competition between military personnel and the private sector to save a dollar. When the savings affected staffing of the desperately needed medical personnel that would be required in a time of war, we were touched personally. These policies worked out in our reality as severe staff shortages. Many qualified medical nurses left by the scores for better pay and a much less traumatic workplace. Others were deployed to the battlefield as the surge continued.

On one hand, we marveled at the skill of the attending doctors, but we were dismayed by the lack of nurses to follow through with the moment by moment care needed by someone with multiple traumas such as Bryan's. Our son was desperately ill. He would have been better served by a continuum of care, yet his complex daily care was managed by various individuals who had never seen him before and often would never see him again. The dwindling supply of remaining nurses did not have the sufficient time required to invest in one patient when their caseload had multiple wounded who needed them with equal intensity. The limited quality nurses were used to staff the day shifts. The staffing of the night shift terrorized me.

The remaining staff was spread ever thinner as the Iraq surge of wounded military personnel increased. It was only a matter of time before serious medical mistakes would occur in Bryan's care.

Chapter 16
LONG DAYS

The first eighteen days of our journey saw our son continuing to fight daily for his life as he faced additional sickness. During these intense days one great joy we continued to witness was incredible healing in our son's mind. He certainly was not living in a vegetative state but was interacting with those around him and his environment. He had not advanced out of the coma, but neither was he sliding back to the lower end of the Glasgow Coma Scale (GCS). He was at eleven and we were filled with hope. Because of Bryan's inability to make his own decisions during this period of time, it was left to us to give permission to the surgeons to remove the lower portion of Bryan's right leg. It was a crushing call for a parent to make, but it was the right decision. His body grew stronger as a result.

During these long days I had stood to the left side of Bryan's body and appealed to God for healing while I massaged his paralyzed hand. I refused to let it curl up and wither. I worked on his arm, all the while talking to him about our love for him.

We were so proud of him. I reassured him that I was there. We were there. God had provided a way for us to be with him. I told Bryan I would not leave him. We would leave together. I reminded him how great a God we had. I told him God had given him, along with us, a message through Psalm 103. These scriptures were for us in our time of need. I recited and prayed it verse by verse, replacing all the personal pronouns with Bryan's name. I did this many times a day. Everyday. I had marveled at God's love that He would invite me to memorize this Psalm. He knew it contained major truths we would need to concentrate on and remember. What if I had refused to obey the inner voice of the Holy Spirit? What then? I hadn't a free hand to hold a Bible. I surely could not have read it to Bryan. I was dismayed to find that my vision had grown dim with suffering from sorrow and grief.

As we prayed for him, his brain began healing to the point he could communicate with us. He had been very determined to communicate and would grow greatly distressed when we failed to comprehend. He tried to talk around the trache with such effort that it made his throat bleed. Bryan had a deep desire to know what had happened to his fellow Marines. Where they hurt? Where they okay? Particularly poignant to me was how clearly I could hear him say "Mama".

He grew frustrated with the gloves I wore. He worked intently to remove them. He would close his eyes in rest when my hand was free, and it rested in his. Skin to skin.

I remember vividly how shocked I was when we came to understand that although Bryan's eyes would open, he could not see. He was blind! Soon we too were blind with tears of comprehension and sorrow.

We quickly established simple signs of communication. Bryan was instructed to give us a thumbs up or down in answer to simple yes or no questions. For questions that required a numerical answer a directed number of eye blinks had been a very effective short-term solution.

We had cried out in utter brokenness to the God who heals, and God restored a measure of sight that same day. It was a spine tingling, incredibly personal miracle to witness his sight return. The commandant of the Marine Corp was there to witness it as Bryan reached to intervene the gifting of a coin and handshake. There was not a dry eye in the room. We had every reason to believe the trache would be removed shortly and trusted that he would be able to talk freely again soon.

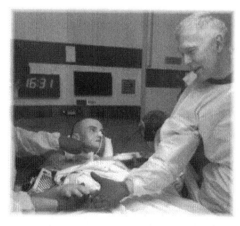

While Bryan receives the coin, he is making eye contact with his visitors.

His body had continued to fight against a raging infection hidden somewhere unknown. His heart was under great strain, and lungs that had been damaged by the blast refused to heal. He had been placed on an every-other-day surgery schedule where they had continued to wash out his wounds. Attempts had been made to surgically repair parts of his damaged body step by step.

Many of these surgeries had been successful, but often these efforts were compromised by the intense fevers, high white cell count and pneumonia in both lungs. So fragile was his grip on life, he slipped away once again while he was in surgery. The use of electric shock resuscitated him and brought him back to us. Bryan came back that day with a new pair of chest tubes as his lungs had collapsed during surgery. I was gravely concerned that he would die. I pleaded with God to heal my boy.

Often, I questioned myself as to my motives for wanting my son to continue to fight so hard to live. I felt mortified at my selfishness as I stood guard and saw his suffering. I wanted him to live. I couldn't bear to think of a life without Bryan. But at what cost? His pain was so debilitating that there wasn't a time when he was not thrashing about trying to find relief. His brain injury affected his body's ability to regulate his body temperature. He wore a special thermal suit that would attempt to bring down his raging fever with an icy coldness that would leave him desperate to find warmth despite his fiery flesh. I felt guilt at my selfishness.

Was I to hold on to my son? Or was I to let go? I begged God to take away his pain but leave my son. The unyielding brutality of his pain began to visit me with horrifying nightmares as I was emotionally bruised and spent by being witness to his uncontrolled suffering.

The steady stream of military coming to pay their respects, along with celebrities, doctors, and nursing staff, intertwined with the constant real time life and death decisions, left us with very little time to attend to essential personal needs.

There were no chairs provided in Bryan's small room. Soon we were all having physical issues from days of long hours standing and infrequent bathroom breaks.

Chapter 17
UNBELIEVABLE NIGHT

The day came when the doctors at the National Naval Medical Center had utilized all their expertise at pain control. They were finally ready to seek help outside the military system of health care. Earlier that day on Thursday, March 22, a call had been placed to an area Pain Specialist. We were encouraged when a local doctor whose specialized field was pain management had agreed to come after his practice closed for the day.

As the evening drew near, we reluctantly slipped out of Bryan's room to grab a quick bite to eat before the cafeteria closed and the endless evening began.

It had been a long and painful day. I was being pulled in conflicting directions. I had been approached to testify before the 2007 Congressional hearings taking place down the hall in the same building we were in. These hearings were televised for the world to hear about the incredible strain on the military hospitals during this distressing time of war.

They wanted a mother's testimony as to the undue hardship our loved heroes were enduring as a result of the lack of quality nursing staff. Daily these shortages endangered the lives of our sons and daughters. Routinely, preventable accidents happened to our wounded warriors that would have shocked and outraged the public as much as it did us, if only they knew. Truthfully, I was desperate for the American public to know. Daily we were doing more and more of the hands-on nursing care ourselves that for which we were not trained. Day by day we were asked to live with the consequences of Congressional and bureaucratic inability to agree and fund the necessary budget.

These resources were needed to provide the daily maintenance and needs of feeding and housing loved ones invited to come by the hundreds to be a part of their warrior's healing. They were running out of places to house us as the surge of wounded heroes increased ensuring the added hardship of an already impossibly hard life experience. How it grieved my heart to see some of these brave men lie in their beds of suffering without one advocate to intercede for them. Someone needed to speak up!

Yet I was in the middle of Bryan's immediate crisis and I was unwilling to leave his side. Hollie had made the decision to go back to Grand Junction to withdraw from her senior year at Mesa State. She returned home to pack up and let her apartment go. She was committed to return to be by her brother's side. Even in the few days that she had been gone her unavailable help was felt to the bone-weary core of our beings.

We hurried back from our hastily eaten meal. Entering the long hall that led to his cubicle on the left, I heard the unmistakable sounds of my son's agony. Suddenly we were cast into a real-life horror show.

Bryan's bed was located directly in front of the nurse's station. There were no doors to impede the line of sight from any angle. The charge nurse was talking on the phone. I had never seen her before.

It had taken Bryan no short amount of time to find himself in serious trouble. He was mere inches off the floor on the left side of his bed. He was secured only by the traction equipment on the right side of the bed that kept his amputated leg partially secure and by a mangled mess of monitor and IV lines. His damaged left leg was hitting the floor along with the pump to which it was attached. It was apparent that his breathing tube was being pulled out by the weight of his body pulling against the ventilator.

Traumatized, I called for the charge nurse's help with urgency. The nurse had no visible concern for our son's predicament. Her only response was to glare at me and talk louder as our son's hoarse agony grew desperate. I was frozen in stunned disbelief.

Craig rushed to Bryan's rescue without suiting up.

Again, I made an effort to get the charge nurse to respond. Unbelievably, as I called out loudly to be heard over the cries of our son, she turned her back on me and continued to talk on the phone. I was astonished at her behavior. It was crystal clear that Bryan was in serious distress and needed immediate intervention.

It was easy to discern that the phone call was of a personal nature. She loudly bantered back and forth with someone on the phone.

"Oh NO you don't, girl!" She laughed into the phone. Don't you be tellin' me that!"

Heads began to appear in doorways close by. Still her conversation continued as she talked about when she got home and so forth. I was stunned! Could this really be happening? What universe was I in?

I looked around in shock and disbelief. Was I having a nightmare? "How could she be so neglectful of her job?" I asked myself. "What should I do?" I looked around for help. There was no one else.

As Bryan's convulsive gasps grew louder, I interrupted her begging for help.

"PLEASE *help us*? PLEASE, PLEASE HELP US!"

Her reaction was to glower at me with what looked like pure evil as her dark eyes bore into mine.

Again, I was shocked and confused. Why would she hate us? She had never met us! I was dumbfounded and shook at her hardness of heart. How could it be that someone so devoid of caring was assigned to be the ICU charge nurse for the night!?

"May God in heaven help us all!" I spoke to myself as I audibly whispered cries for God's intervention. Passionately I continued to request help.

Eventually she slammed the phone down in utter contempt at me. She was enraged. How DARE I interrupt her when she was on the phone! She had a RIGHT to talk on the phone! NO ONE was gonna tell her she couldn't talk on the PHONE! Again, I pointed to my son in dismay and begged for someone to help. Icily she informed me that SHE was the charge nurse and as such SHE would decide who needed what and when. She informed me further that she had a long list of responsibilities and she would decide when and IF she had time to help our son.

Looking around at the people that had been drawn into our crisis she made more scathing remarks that left us all speechless as she continued her tantrum. She sent colleagues that were witnesses to her behavior scurrying to their assignments. It was obvious she intimidated them.

I didn't know who she was, but I knew she had crossed an ethical line. We were left to tend to Bryan ourselves as she refused to help. How could she abuse her position of authority like she was? I was appalled!

Physically shaken to the core, we cried out to God for help. Within minutes the Pain Specialist walked in upon our unimaginable predicament. He helped us get Bryan re-attached to all of his equipment. As we worked side by side with him, he questioned us as to what had just happened. With an air of authority, he assured us that he would handle the situation. He attempted to introduce himself to the charge nurse.

With a complete lack of professionalism, she completely ignored him. She wouldn't even look at him. He made repeated requests for her attention to no avail.

He tried another approach. He told her the equipment and medicines he would need to relieve Bryan of his obvious pain.

This drew her wrath.

She forcefully informed him that SHE didn't work for him.

IF he needed anything, he could get it HIMSELF!

Truly it was the most alarming and disheartening experience we had had thus far. I was physically shaking with shock as I watched her continue to refuse to help the doctor or my son in ANY way. Evil with a dark heart was in charge of the ICU.

The visiting doctor was at a serious disadvantage and charge nurse knew it. This was a military hospital and the Pain Specialist was not on staff. He didn't know where the needles and syringes were kept. He didn't know the procedure to procure the medicines he needed to make the pain cocktail for Bryan. For Pete's sake, he didn't even know where the cotton balls and bandages were!!

I began to pray that God would be the doctor's helper. After an agonizing amount of time and a few quick phone calls made by the Pain Specialist, one of the doctors on Bryan's medical team showed up. Together they were able to procure the supplies needed to help our son.

As the clock inched closer to 11:00 p.m. we dreaded to leave our son in the care of this charge nurse.

I felt her vengeful stares upon us. As I stood by Bryan's bed, I waited to see who his individual night nurse would be. Moments before the 11:00 p.m. curfew, his nurse walked in his room.

She was not a military nurse but was from a pool of nurses they often hired when they had a shortage. We parents called them Rent-A-Nurses. We were on full alert when our sons were under their care. Tonight, of all nights, Bryan had a Rent-A-Nurse.

In an effort to bring her up to speed on Bryan's condition in the few remaining moments we had, I soon discovered she didn't speak English. It was truly a mind-numbing shock! The implications were unthinkable! This was my son's life that hung in the balance!

My body shook in horror as I was traumatized. We were in the National Naval Medical Center in Bethesda, Maryland, USA, and the nurse didn't speak English!?? Could the night get any more bizarre or terrifying??

Surely, she could at the very least understand English?? I told her it was extremely important that she understood me.

"Do NOT turn off Bryan's feeding tube." I said.

"DO NOT turn off his feeding tube, he is on *insulin*." I repeated with explanation.

I told her this with words and with hand signals. I told her Bryan was going into surgery in the early morning. If he were a normal case it would be proper to turn off his feeding tube so that he would not get stomach upset. However, because Bryan had to go into surgery so often, they inserted the feeding tube below the stomach. This avoided the constant threat of stomach upset and the disruption of calories his body so desperately needed for the healing process.

Did she understand me? Surely, she understood. She was a nurse after all.

Craig and I left the hospital at the closing of visiting hours unsure of whether communication had occurred. Despite being extremely tired and emotionally spent it was impossible to sleep. The trauma of the evening lingered freshly in our bodies. We sensed something was gravely wrong and spent most of the night crying out in whispered anguished prayers for our son.

As both peace and sleep continued to elude me even with my sleeping pill, Craig slipped out into the night.

Singularly focused he made his way back to Bryan's bedside. Comforted that Craig was going to check on our son, I fell into a troubled sleep.

Chapter 18
A NEW FRONTLINE

Craig slipped into the National Naval Medical Center and hurried to the ICU to find the doors to the floor locked. Looking through the narrow window in the door separating him from the hall leading to Bryan's ICU side, he witnessed a flurry of activity in and out of what appeared to be Bryan's room.

As he continued to watch Craig held on to hope that the apparent emergency was NOT our son.

As countless numbers of medical personnel continued to rush to the scene, Craig slipped through the door in the wake of a nurse. Surrounding Bryan's bedside were multiple doctors and medical personnel. They were in the process of trying to resuscitate our son.

Bryan's body was completely motionless.

No one even tried to explain the unexplainable to Craig. His presence was barely acknowledged as he stood in the shadow of unfolding events.

Bryan's blood sugar was *zero*. His feeding tube had been shut off. His insulin pump had been left on. He had a hypoglycemic event caused by nursing error.

As they scrambled to reverse the deadly effects of low blood sugar, Bryan's body refused to respond. Our son who had been interacting with us just hours before was now given a lower Glasgow Coma Scale number than when he was flown in from the battlefield of Iraq!

He now had a score of *three*, the lowest score given. There was *no* brain activity. He had suffered another devastating brain injury. He was on life support. For the next several hours the medical team rushed to reverse the effects of the insulin overdose. Craig stood silently praying in the shadows, listening, observing, and believing God for the life of our son. God was our son's only hope.

They followed protocol and administered measured doses of D50 in intervals racing through hours to bring his blood sugar back up. Still Bryan's body was unresponsive. Because of this, they quickly made the decision to take him off all pain medications. This included any medication that might have a sedative effect. Still Bryan lay motionless and unresponsive.

Next the decision was made to administer drugs to counteract the narcotics he had been given the evening before. Despite all these measures, Bryan continued to lay unresponsive to any type of brutal pain inflicted on his body.

There was no other medical plan for the foreseeable hours. They would wait to see what his motionless body would do.

Prying my sleep deprived and emotionally spent, drugged body from bed I hastily dressed and made my way through the corridor of the Navy Lodge where we were currently staying. Over the course of the eighteen days that we had been in Washington, D.C., we had been moved three times. These changes left me in a constant state of confusion as to where I was physically in relation to Bryan's room.

Getting to Bryan's bedside was no simple task. The long walk to find a familiar entrance gave me precious minutes to commit the yet unforeseen events of the day into the keeping of the Lord.

I entered the long hall of the ICU with cautious optimism. Prayerfully the new pain medications would have given our warrior long sought-after relief.

In the course of suiting up to go into Bryan's cubicle, I had a vague but powerful sense that something was not right. My eyes went back and forth from my son to my husband. Craig had his back to me. He hesitated when I called his name. In the stillness of those moments I became aware that my husband was trying to compose himself. I saw devastation etched into his face as he slowly turned toward me as my eyes sought and found my son. He was completely motionless. In an instant my perception that his lack of movement meant effective pain management was shattered. In perpetual slow motion I comprehended that Bryan was on total life support. I stood frozen as the reality of what my eyes beheld conflicted with the certain knowledge that God was in control. I had no way of knowing what had happened during the night to bring about so grave an outcome, but I knew our angst in the night was validated. In those hard moments I chose to believe that God was not just simply standing watch over the surreal events of the hours past, He was at work. He was using the works of the enemy somehow — maybe to strengthen the resolve we had as parents to intensify our prayers for our son — maybe to reveal that we had entered a spiritual battle for the life of our son.

God was actively at work in the life of my only son. I fiercely believed this! I couldn't see at that moment what He was doing, but He was working all things together for our good and for His glory. I was certain.

I was alarmed at the great hatred displayed by the devil's schemes. The charge nurse had allowed herself to be used as a pawn in the enemy's pursuit to destroy our son. We had watched in horror and disbelief as she used her position of authority to deny our son help. Her callousness, lack of professionalism and care set off a chain reaction that resulted in an overdose of insulin that gravely injured our son's brain.

In those ensuing hours I battled to forgive her and leave her actions to be judged by others so that I could move forward. I would not trust her again nor would I accept her behavior.

I did not have energy or time to pursue revenge, and it clearly was not my place to do so. I placed my hot anger in God's hands and asked Him to help me to be focused on what He was doing in our lives through these unbelievable days.

The events of the evening before and the following hours on that Friday were nightmarish. Oddly the nursing staff didn't even come into his room. They would pass by glancing in covertly. Not once did they volunteer to explain the grave error that was made the night before. We were left alone in grief standing guard over our son as he lay motionless on life support. The apparent callousness of the staff added to our grief and confusion.

From the beginning days at Bethesda Craig and I had many questions that we longed to discuss together, yet alone time was just nonexistent. We had concluded weeks prior that we would never discuss our troubled feelings and thoughts in Bryan's presence. He would only hear us — if he could hear us — discuss his progress with truth and compassion. In those heartbreaking hours we surrounded him and ourselves with prayer, praise music and the written word of God.

The Lord is my light and my salvation — whom shall I fear?
The Lord is the stronghold of my life — of whom shall I be afraid?

*When evil men advance against me to devour my flesh,
when my enemies and my foes attack me, they will stumble
and fall.*
*Though an army besiege me, my heart will not fear;
Though war break out against me, even then will I be
confident. . . .*
*For in the day of trouble he will keep me safe in his
dwelling; he will hide me in the shelter of his tabernacle
and set me high upon a rock.*
*Then my head will be exalted above the enemies who
surround me; at his tabernacle will I sacrifice with shouts
of joy;*
I will sing and make music to the LORD.
*Hear my voice when I call, O LORD; be merciful to me
and answer me...*
I am still confident of this:
*I will see the goodness of the LORD in the land of the
living.*
*Wait for the LORD; be strong and take heart and wait
for the LORD.*
Psalms 27:1-3, 5-7, 13-14 (NIV)

We committed again our belief that all things were possible
with God. We looked to Him to act. We did not trust in man.

As the day progressed, we pieced together a small
understanding of what was taking place behind the scene.

There was an investigation taking place about the events of
the last twenty-four hours. Dr. Liston had called a meeting of
all personnel and had expressed his outrage that something of

this magnitude would happen to a Marine whose life they had been entrusted with. There he relieved the charge nurse of her duty in the ICU, but he was unable to fire her because she was a governmental employee.

When Dr. Liston finally came in to see Bryan, he too was strangely quiet. As he left the room, I followed him down the hall. There I implored him to explain to me in simple terms what had happened to my son during the night.

Taking a deep breath, he said it was as if someone had taken a sledgehammer to Bryan's brain. There was no appreciable chance of survival. His descriptive language gave me a stunning visual. I was left without voice to question any further. The injury was grave. Our son had no response whatsoever. None. Bryan was at 3 on the Glasgow Coma scale. A vegetative state. He was so very sorry.

Immediately my thoughts scrambled back to what I knew of the Glasgow Coma scale. It is a diagnostic tool that medical practitioners use to diagnose symptoms of Traumatic Brain Injury. The test measured the motor response, verbal response and eye-opening response. The lowest response in each category is a 1 which translates to no response. Bryan had no response to all three categories — 1+1+1=3. Today our son had a score of 3.

Thursday when we left for the night, he had a score of 11. Clearly our son had been injured apart from the injuries of war. I returned to Bryan's side immediately, freshly devastated, but with a full understanding of what we needed to do. We needed to ask God to bring life into our son's brain. We needed to believe God could and would do the impossible. For Him nothing was impossible.

It was also imperative that we stay by his side at night from now on. Never would we leave him again. In faith we cried out for God to intervene and speak healing into our son's brain.

We notified our family with the devastating news of his latest injury and our immediate family prepared to come. Hollie cut her trip home short and booked an immediate flight back to D.C. She would arrive Saturday evening March 24. Our daughter Jennifer and son-in-law Isaiah jumped in our car in Delta, Colorado, and began the 1,936-mile trek to Washington, DC.

As the evening continued, I was further disheartened and wounded to read the report the charge nurse wrote concerning the night before.

Her report was full of shameless lies that placed the full blame on me, Bryan's mother. She reported that I came back from supper and woke my peacefully sleeping son. She wrote that I proceeded to put him through rigorous range of motion exercises that caused him to need pain care intervention.

My heart plunged within me as I came to realize the full extent of the evil plaguing my son's life that she would lie in black print so brazenly. I was allowed to read further entries that the charge nurse had included in her report that very morning. Could these lies be the reason the nursing staff was reluctant to enter Bryan's room? Did they believe her lies?

Everything was date and time stamped in the computer. Information could not be manipulated or changed, yet she had tried with her handwritten notes. I was promptly assured by the outraged doctor that had allowed me to read those notes that her attempts to rewrite history only served to magnify her guilt.

The timeline showed that shortly after we left for the night Bryan's feeding tube was shut off. His insulin drip continued running. There were no further entries till he was found unresponsive in the early morning hours. The evidence showed that Bryan received none of his scheduled care or meds during the night time hours.

The fact that he had not received the medicines or human touch he so desperately needed filled me with grief. My mind could not comprehend how it was possible that this had happened to someone so deathly sick. Wouldn't it stand to reason that you would monitor them closer?

I remembered the charge nurse's animosity. Had this been intentional and not an error?

It was beyond belief that Bryan had survived an IED blast in Iraq only to be in peril in this place of healing. I felt righteous anger rising to the surface. NEVER, despite the rules, would he be left alone again.

For the previous three days our son had been in incredible pain. The intense pain had required mega doses of painkillers and nothing had worked. Now as I stood watch over my son, he showed no outward signs of pain that would show life within.

I struggled with the knowledge that he had been off those powerful pain meds for sixteen hours and still lay silent. The haunting truth could be that he was in incredible misery. The physicians were counting on the intense buried pain to awaken his body from the deep vegetative state. They would come in periodically to inflict him with brutal measures to elicit pain in hopes of a response. We were helpless to do anything but stand guard. We waited, crying out to our God for His mercy of intervention and healing.

I studied Bryan computerized chart that had been left on.

It was usually full of instruction about the care and medicines to be given. There was a simple, three-word sentence written by Dr. Liston.

DO NO HARM.

I wept, broken in mind and body.

Craig was given permission to stay that night with our son. He would have to continue to stand attention as not a single chair was provided in the small ICU room.

The next morning, I found my way back to Bryan's side to relieve my husband. He had not left Bryan's bedside since he had slipped through the door on that unbelievable night. He had been standing guard for 29 traumatic hours.

Three weeks prior we had been assigned a Marine officer who would be by our side during some of our worst moments.

Parker's duty was to attend to our concerns and help us navigate the military system.

Over the course of the previous emotionally intense weeks, I became close to a dear lady who was a type of surrogate mother to our young Marine officer. Pam was the manager of the Navy exchange, NEX, on the base. She had come to visit me while I stood by Bryan several times in the past.

On that Saturday morning after I had been with Bryan for a couple hours Pam showed up as if on cue. Bryan's body had begun to jerk and twitch ever so slowly. Soon it was all I could do to keep his convulsing body from falling out of bed. As tears fell, I cried softly for Jesus to send help. I looked up and Pam was there.

God had heard my whispered pleadings and sent me help. He knew I needed more than help. I needed a friend. He also heard the groaning of my heart to comprehend the truths He was teaching me in these intensely tender times. He knew that my confidence could not rest in the abilities of great physicians and great institutions to heal my son. He knew how deeply they had wounded my trust. My confidence must rest in the one true Great Physician.

Pam stayed all that Saturday helping me with my son. She took one side. I took the other. Together our bodies were visibly battered and severely bruised as we wrestled with Bryan's body to keep him from hurting himself. His violent seizures lasted into the evening and beyond. Not one member of the medical personnel physically helped me with my son all day.

That Saturday evening when visiting hours ended, we were asked to leave. We had understood that one person from our family would be permitted to stay. We were tersely told that we were mistaken. We would have to leave.

I painfully regretted leaving on that unbelievable night of Thursday, March 22. I certainly was not going to make the same mistake twice. To be called upon to leave my son in his current medical condition was unconscionable. The day had come to take a stand.

I respectfully but firmly refused to leave my son's bedside. The result was to be repeatedly coerced and shamed verbally by a female officer of high rank. When several hours of this tactic failed to have the desired results, she threatened me with arrest. I assured the whole lot of them quite adamantly that I would be staying with my son. As the military police were called to take me away, I stood my ground. With a deep sense of dismay at the lack of compassion shown toward our family during our deep sorrow, I wondered what had happened to the America that I knew. I was a mother of a physically devastated Marine freshly injured on their watch. To be hauled off to jail for attempting to protect the trace of life that was left in my son's battered body was indefensible. I had entrusted him to the hospital's care many nights. But NO more! I was NOT leaving! I firmly stated that I was not leaving my son! One of us WOULD be staying! After long tense minutes the MPs were visibly relieved to stand down when orders came from a position of even higher, saner authority. In the end Craig was allowed to stay and stand guard over our son's precious body.

When I finally made my way back to the room under the cover of darkness, I was horrified that I had almost been arrested for standing up for the right to protect my injured Marine son. What kind of place was this that they bully mothers?

The events of the day threatened to crush the very life out of my chest. I had some idea of the effects of physical and emotional trauma on the human body. I had suffered as a child, but I was an adult now! I was dismayed that many of my old fears were rushing in. I took the sleeping pill the doctor insisted would drive away the nightmares and sobbed myself to sleep.

Chapter 19
THE STORM

When I returned Sunday morning, I was greatly encouraged to discover that our daughter Jennifer and our son-in-law Isaiah had arrived. They were fully engaged in Bryan's care. Hollie Mae had arrived the evening before along with Bryan's Uncle Jeff.

Craig and I were visibly relieved to have reinforcements to stand physically against the powers of darkness on behalf of our beloved son. We all gathered around him in his room. We prayed for his healing and deliverance from the onslaught of disaster. I was encouraged by the observable love, commitment and faith our family members displayed for their brother and nephew. We were refreshed by their presence.

God would do amazing exploits in the night time hours. Hollie Mae wrote the following on the Caringbridge.org website.

Dear Family and Friends,

The Lord delights in those who fear Him, in those who put their hope in His unfailing love." Psalm 147:1 (NIV)

Today we are reminded again of God's unfailing and immeasurable love for His children. He never lets us get too far from Him and He listens to our prayers and is MIGHTY to save.

Bryan was fully awake once again! Last night I stayed with him until about four in the morning and at 1AM he "woke" up and was nodding his head and answering questions with hand squeezes and eye blinks. This is so amazing! We never doubted that God would heal Bryan (again), but we were impressed from the start that we would have to "wait" and practice our patience.

The only sad part in this latest healing is that Bryan had forgotten about his leg. Last night when he was very awake, he was doing all the checking out of his parts to reassure himself that they were all there. He was getting so agitated with his legs and moving them both around alot so I had to ask him if he wanted me to tell him about his legs. I told him to open his eyes and look at me if he wanted me to tell him. He opened both eyes and looked right at me — so I told him (again). It never gets any easier and for Bryan it was like learning about it for the first time — he wasn't happy. I am praying that he allows God to use this in his life and in the life of those praying for him, that God would draw Bryan and all of us closer to Him.

Thank you for your prayers, support and love for Bryan — he's going to be just fine. We serve a powerful God,

one who loves us, loves Bryan, and will not let anyone or anything frustrate the plans He has made for Bryan's life. Praise, Glory and Honor to our Father!
Love and Grateful Thanks, The Chambers

By the time I awoke and returned to the hospital on that early Monday morning Bryan had slipped back into a much lower level of consciousness.

I relished and mentally relived the accounts Hollie told about her conversations with Bryan during the night. Oh, how I wished I would have been there! To witness his awakening would have been like seeing Lazarus opening his eyes from death! I was so encouraged by the kindness of God that revealed our son was still very much with us, should he escape from the coma that kept pulling him back as prisoner. God had once again moved in his mysterious ways and gave us life with hope.

It was difficult to comprehend that Bryan could slide back and forth on the Glascow Coma Scale (GCS) when he closed his eyes in sleep. I hung on to the hope that he would awaken again. We prayed for the time it would be complete and permanent. As the day progressed it was obvious that his life was in peril once again.

His pain level became uncontrollable. His white blood cell count was extremely elevated, and his flesh burnt to the touch. How much more could his heart withstand? He was taken quickly to the OR for emergency surgery.

As we waited, we made the smaller of the two waiting rooms our altar of prayer. We knelt as a family to ask God to spare his life once again. The intense pain and infection appeared to be in his extremely sensitive private area. We pleaded with our sovereign God to heal him and to allow Bryan to retain the ability to father children.

The news came back that surgery was over. I would be allowed to go back and see my son soon. We praised God that once again Bryan's life was spared.

Needing to find a solitary place to be alone, I sought the shelter of a distant deserted hallway. It was there that Dr. Liston found me and broke the news that the decision had been made to remove Bryan's only remaining testicle. There would be no babies. In that moment of time while I was awash in uncontrolled raw grief, Dr. Liston discarded his role as a highly decorated military physician and gathered me into fatherly arms. Together we sobbed loudly for the costly sacrifice made by a young Marine and his family.

Not once did I ever imagine that my Father God was indifferent to our emotional pain. Though others could study our outward appearance and see the signs of grief this latest sacrifice produced, only God knew the deep hurt we felt to the marrow of our bones. It was a confounding mystery to me as God's child that my Father would decree this outcome for my only son.

I thought back over the events of the last weeks and charted the highs and lows like a graph on the volatile New

York Stock Exchange. There had been incredible highs, but as the arrow plunged creating a deep chasm, I was confronted with questions so troubling I was speechless. I needed time and space to be alone with this sovereign God that I suddenly feared. He had spoken as out of a Holy mountain and I was terrified.

I had seen God raise my son from the dead as if Bryan was a modern-day Lazarus. I saw Him perform repeated astounding saves. Would I now grow suspicious when He chose not to heal?

I returned to Bryan's bedside early Tuesday morning for the changing of the guard. Though he showed no signs of alertness, I talked to him softly and reassured him of my presence. I quoted our personal Psalm to him and prayed for him and our family. I wept.

As I positioned his ear phones so that he could be encouraged by praise music and to mask the sounds of my sadness, I thought about the good-byes we said the night before. Our cherished family members that had come to offer relief had been there during a most crucial time. We saw the hand of God in their help and in their interceding on behalf of Bryan's life.

It had been emotionally tough to see our daughter Jennifer and son-in-law Isaiah go, but never had we been so convinced that their place was back at home with their little ones that they had left behind. Life was so uncertain. So fragile. The short ones needed their parents at home. They would come again if we needed them. We were certain.

That Monday Craig and I received an invitation to meet with the Admiral of the Navy where we obtained permission to stay with our son 24/7. While deeply desired, the necessity of night time coverage created an incredible hardship for our family. Craig and I had long since sacrificed our times of intimate aloneness to the effects of sleeping pills and the presence of an adult daughter we shared a room with. Now we would no longer have moments of comfort received from simply sleeping near each other in the night.

Technically we divided the 24 hours into three 8-hour shifts with Craig always taking the night shift. In reality we often overlapped our shifts and spent long wakeful hours on our feet together.

Hollie took the night shift that first Monday night to give her Dad some much needed rest. She wrote the following entry in Caringbridge.

Hey everybody!

Another semi-rough night with Bryan. His feeding tube had to be re-inserted through his nose (ouch), Bryan did not appreciate the doctors who did this. After waiting about a half an hour for the tube to be carried down in his gut by his digestive tract they had to x-ray his abdomen to make sure the tube was in the correct spot and wait for the slides to come back — then he got some medicine! Whew… Bryan and I were both worn out by this time.

He had been running a temp and his body fights so hard against that ice vest that the nurse decided to turn it off and allow the fever to run its course naturally. Bryan hates that vest so I know he slept better without it. His fever did spike to about 100.9 before it broke leaving Bryan clammy and soaking wet. I spent the rest of the night monitoring his pain level through questions that he would respond to and wiping down his face and arms as the fever came down. Pain was a little hard to regulate as he would be sleeping fairly smoothly then start awake and grab at some different part that was hurting him — namely his legs and lower abdomen. Once he would do that it was pretty easy to ask if he was in pain (kind of a "no duh" when you are having to hold him down) and request more meds from the nurse.

All in all, it was a fairly good night. I remain very encouraged that Bryan is so responsive (i.e. "Bryan will you turn your head so I can put your earphones in?" To which he promptly turns his head for me). God is very faithful and very good. Please pray for Bryan's pain level again- it is manageable and treatable but they are rightfully trying not to give him too many meds, Bryan has to wake up enough to demonstrate pain level before they'll give him another dose.

The dosages are fairly fast acting but it's at least 20 mins where Bryan is in pain and that is hard to watch. I told Bryan that if he had to go through it so bravely that the least I could do was stand there with him and try to be equally as tough. But it is hard!

We very much appreciate everyone's prayers — we say it every time we post, and we mean it every time we post-

151

you are a blessing to us and we are praying back God's presence and favor on each of your lives. We will write more later…
Love and thanks, Hollie Chambers

Isaiah 41:13 *"For I am the Lord your God, who takes hold of your right hand and says to you, Do not fear; I will help you."* (NIV)

I had renewed hope as the morning progressed. We were being moved to the 5th floor! Craig would be astounded to find us there when he came back after lunch. I knew the reasoning behind the move. They HAD to get us out of ICU. No one should be witness to the night shift in ICU and be able to tell about it.

I continued to believe that Bryan's body would heal and grow stronger. The infectious area that had been driving up his pain level had been surgically attended to, I reasoned. That painful and very emotional surgery was behind us. We would look forward.

I ached to see him relieved of pain that still seemed to increase as the minutes inched toward his morning bath time. Would his pain ever end?

Two young Navy Corpsmen entered the room chatting happily as they prepared Bryan for his much-needed bath. Bath time was not his favorite as it required a lot of painful repositioning of his fragile body.

I stood looking into my son's anxious face as I reassured him and held his right shoulder toward me as they turned him on his left side. He could never be turned to the right side as that side bore the grisly looking external fixator that kept his shattered femur in place. The apparatus bore multiple pins that protruded from his flesh and were attached to four long metal rods running the length of his femur. The external fixator was very heavy. Despite the doctors hope to replace it with an internal fixation, Bryan had continued to be too sick for the procedure.

In an attempt to thoroughly clean Bryan, one of them held his damaged leg fairly high as the other Corpsman washed him.

After he had received a vigorous cleansing the Corpsman thoughtlessly dropped his injured leg. His amputated right leg slammed heavy with the external fixator against his swollen scrotal sack. The contents *exploded* wetness all over, covering my face and clothes.

I was stunned, traumatized with horror! I will never forget the look of excruciating pain on Bryan's face as his eyes locked on mine. He screamed through his trache in raw agony. His body convulsing with unimaginable trauma. I couldn't contain my horror and sorrow at the pain he felt as I fell to the floor still clinging to his shoulder.

Quick to avert their own dread and responsibility, they started to minimize the harm done to Bryan by telling me over and over that he was okay.

He certainly wasn't okay! I released his shoulder, stood up and passionately revealed to them their handiwork. "Look at me! Look at my face!" I wailed as I wiped my son's tissue from my cheek. "Look at my clothes! Look at my son!!"

Bryan was inconsolable and so was I. How could this happen? I agonized. Why did it happen? It was as if the enemy kicked us both in our deepest wounds.

Again, I sank to the side of his bed and held his anguished face in my hands as we sobbed in unison.

Quickly the young girls gathered the towels and wash basin and fled from the room.

I pulled the emergency cord and waited for the nurse to come.

Once again, the extent of his injury was diminished. The nurse gave him additional pain meds and said she would contact the doctor.

Several hours passed unaided. I anxiously waited for Craig to awaken and come to us. He usually came around one o'clock in the afternoon. He never knew what awaited his arrival. Almost all of Bryan's scheduled procedures happened in the early morning hours while he was asleep.

I had been softly praying for help when I happened to see the urologist pass down the hall. I called his name and hurried down the corridor. He had several of his associates with him. I convinced him that he needed to come see my son. I told of the injury Bryan had endured.

He took one look at Bryan hemorrhaging into his bed coverings. Taking immediate control of the situation he personally rolled Bryan in his bed out of his room and rushed him to the OR. Bryan was in surgery for over 5 hours.

Overnight with each beat of his heart there was a small leak from a blood vessel they tied off during yesterday's painful surgery. The doctor called it a tumor. The tumor had grown to the size of a grapefruit extending into his scrotal sac. This is what exploded when the corpsman dropped his leg. Sorrowfully, the damage to Bryan's private area was so extensive the surgeons decided it could not be surgically closed. It would remain open and require months of daily, painful cauterization to heal.

While Bryan was in surgery, Orthopedics came in to do some adjusting on his femur ex-fix. It must have moved some when his leg was dropped. I was assured that his leg was "mostly" set and that the bone could now mend like it should.

Returning to my room that evening, I read the following prayer written on Bryan's Caringbridge site by a dear prayer warrior:

Mighty God and Everlasting Father,
May the Prince of Peace who through His Holy Spirit dwells with Bryan and his family bring them rest this night.
May the Great Physician lay his healing hands upon Bryan and all who lie on beds of affliction around him and the world.

May the Wonderful Counselor give insight to those whose healing knowledge becomes the point of contact between You and the sick and injured...so the wonder of your love might be seen everywhere.

I pray that the cause of Bryan's pain has been found. I ask that his legs and other injuries might rapidly heal...that his bones might heal so quickly that none can doubt you are the reason. Please cure the fever...the pneumonia...any head injuries.

Renew Bryan's spirit. Father, may he rise on Eagle's Wings and run without growing faint.

There is nothing beyond Your power to perform... may our prayers for Bryan lie directly on center within the circle of your will for him and all.

Jesus, we ask these things in Your name...AMEN!

As I knelt beside my bed I was ministered to by songs in the night. Words written by others but felt from the deepest places of my soul.

God, my God I cry out
Your beloved needs you now
God be near, calm my fear
And take my doubt
Your kindness is what pulls me up
Your love is all that draws me in
I will lift my eyes to the Maker
Of the mountains I can't climb

I will lift my eyes to the Calmer
Of the oceans raging wild
I will lift my eyes to the Healer
Of the hurt I hold inside
I will lift my eyes, lift my eyes to You

God, my God, let Mercy sing
Her melody over me God, right here all I bring
Is all of me
Your kindness is what pulls me up
Your love is what draws me in

I will lift my eyes to the Maker
Of the mountains I can't climb
I will lift my eyes to the Calmer
Of the oceans raging wild
I will lift my eyes to the Healer
Of the wounds I hold inside
I will lift my eyes, lift my eyes to You

'Cause You are and You were and You will be forever
The Lover I need to save me
'Cause You fashioned the earth and
  You hold it together, God
So hold me now

God, my God, I cry out
Your beloved needs you now

I Will Lift My Eyes — Bebo Norman[2]

I lay my head down with certainty that my beloved husband was standing guard along with the mighty angels who do God's bidding. (Psalm 103) Still the terror of the day caused my body to shake with uncontrollable tremors as I relived the horror of my son's wounding. Sobbing with sorrow at memories that haunted, I took my hated sleeping pill. I drifted in thought. I was no longer able to read for all the tears that fell unceasingly, still it brought me comfort to clutch my worn Bible to my chest as I drifted off to sleep. I was comforted by thoughts of scripture memorized and the prayers and petitions that were being presented to the Father on our behalf. My prayers had been reduced to consist of three words, "Jesus help us." Darkness consumed me.

Morning came as if in an instant. Prying my drugged eyes open I hastily dressed and made my way through the corridor of the Navy Lodge where we were currently staying.

We had been moved away from the noisy helipad outside our room at The Fisher House. The incoming flights that brought wounded warriors home came in under cover of night. This nightly occurrence had been interpreted by my terrorized brain as incoming enemy forces intent on completing the mission of killing my son. They had weapons and were closing in on me as I tried to drag my son's shattered body up the stairs to safety. He was so heavy. I tried so hard to hide him. I would scream out in terror as they thrust their knives into my flesh. Such were the nightmares that interrupted my family's sleep and necessitated my use of sleeping pills from the earliest of days there. I was saddened and at a loss as to why I could not sleep in peace without them. The doctor said we would deal with that issue later. It was important that I had sleep. My son and family needed me, and I needed rest.

Getting to Bryan's bedside was never a simple task. With the limited number of parking spaces even with a nearby parking garage, the search for a space that morning kept me driving further away than I intended. I saw that the parking garage had been roped off and wondered at the cause. Only later would I be told that a distraught wounded hero had jumped to his death from the top of the garage.

I was honored to be part of the hands-on care for our son.

It was March 28. One month to the date that our world had been altered. As I looked back, I was deeply moved and humbled by all the Father had accomplished in our lives. He had been faithful to supply just what we needed every day, and His presence was tangible to all who entered Bryan's room.

Craig had written an entry in Caringbridge that encouraged my heart. We passed like ships in the night and often the only way I knew how he was holding up was to read his entries. It reminded me of our time as camp counselors where we communicated by passing notes.

Wednesday March 28, 11:25 AM

Craig wrote:

Mornin' y'all, What an incredibly blue-sky day here in the shadow of our nation's capital. Nearing the peak of cherry blossoms. The amazing details of our Creator God never ceases to confound my tired mind. Sorry we couldn't respond earlier with the good news. But sleep has been in short supply around here. I have elected to do the "midnight shift" and my body thinks I am crazy. So, I, like Paul, l am beating my body into subjection. There is a reason God made the darkness, but honestly, I am enjoying the fight.

Words do not seem to be quite adequate tools to describe the joy we have had around here the past 12 hours. Our Father God has shown up here and in the OR and did miracles yet again on our behalf. He is answering every prayer of everyone, from far and wide to young and old.

Our God is a God of details and He has not missed any. I have lost count of the number of large manila envelopes stuffed full of cards written by 1st through 6th graders. Trust me it's the type of stuff David Letterman would pay big bucks to use on his show. But it is all precious to us and extremely precious to our Almighty Everlasting God. All of us could use a dose of their faith, of course God already told us that. He actually places a premium on the faith of a child, I somehow believe their prayers have a certain weight to them that us old timers can only hope to have.

Bryan is fighting back from the fog of surgery like the fighter he is. Rebounding and bouncing back is not reserved for only "Tigger" but it's the M.O. of every Marine. It's

what they do best — they fight back at whatever comes their way. He has a long road ahead, as we all do. But God is in control and on the march to bring him out of this with great Glory and Almighty Power.
More to come, Miracles abound!!!
Bryan's daddo

Craig wrote another entry dated later that same day. I remain so thankful for his ability to put thought to paper. My husband ministered to me by his written words that I could read and re-read. It wasn't the same as private conversation desperately needed, but it met a deep need.

He posted it to the Caringbridge site on Thursday, March 29, 2007, at 11:16 AM.

To: The Faithful Gathered All Around — March 28, 2007 I have been wanting to write to you all since last Friday. God has been on the move so much and doing such extraordinary acts that I can't seem to process fast enough. So I have a lot to share. (Humor Me)
"Here is the point: God is in the resumé building business. He is always using past experiences to prepare us for future opportunities. But those God-given opportunities often come as man-eating lions. And how we react when we encounter those lions will determine our destiny. We can cower in fear and run away from our greatest challenges, OR we can chase our God-ordained destiny by seizing the God-ordained opportunity. As I look back on my own life, I recognize this simple truth — the greatest opportunities were the scariest lions."[3] Mark Batterson,

pastor of NCC in Washington, D.C. (Hollie and I have been attending this church while here in DC).

One other quote that has been running around in my head has been so true this past week- "Good and bad run on parallel tracks in our lives and they usually arrive at about the same time." (Ron Dunn) This is exactly what has been happening around here. Through ALL of it God is being glorified! This quote is actually rooted in Joseph's life when he stated: "What you meant for evil in my life God intended it for good." Please allow me to defend this position with the following observations from the Unbelievable Night (U.N.)

Brief timeline:
8 pm Thursday, 23 – Bryan was in incredible pain and we had the run in with the Charge Nurse, U.N.
8 am Friday, 24 – Bryan was in an Insulin Induced deep coma state (level 3 on a scale of 3 to 15) due to a human error from the night shift
Saturday, 25 – Bryan had been in a deep coma state since Friday with no movement but by afternoon he went through long hours of delirium, thrashing around, raising up. Pulling at things. This lasted almost 24 hours. Sunday – Bryan "wakes" up!!
1) On the U.N. our family's faith was tested to the breaking point. It was our crisis of belief; Satan's biggest gut punch in this month-long chapter of our lives. I was so proud of our family here and our greater global family of faith! Though it was shaken to its very foundations — our faith soared to new heights, to greater levels. As I have glibly stated so many times, "A faith untested rarely ever

grows." Let there be no doubt, God hears every word we ever speak — Be careful what you say! Satan 0 – God 1

2) God used that U.N. to reset Bryan's pain meter. He had been on obscene amounts of morphine and still out of control pain. But coming out of that U.N. he went 24 hours without a single drop of pain meds. Today he is on a much lower dosage of painkillers with much better pain control. Satan 0 – God 2

3) God knew Bryan was going to face another 2 days in the OR for totally unplanned surgeries. He knew that Bryan's body would need rest for these surgeries. His coma days were likely the best sleep he had gotten in weeks as well as keeping the pain and fever under control these days. Satan 0 – God 3

4) God used the U.N. to reawaken a higher level of praying. It was the defining moment we began to see this as a spiritual battle of eternal proportions. We changed the way we had been praying and many of you all did as well. Some of you may even be new to the concept of spiritual warfare – and it was a brief introduction to Reality 101 of the Christian life. Satan has a plan for every one of us- to kill, steal and destroy. We choose to cling to God's offer of LIFE, not just ordinary life but ABUNDANT life! Bryan got caught in the crossfire and you all prayed him though one of his greatest battles! Thank you! Satan 0 – God 4

5) God is using our U.N. to effect change in future Marines and their treatment here at this fine facility. Adjustments and corrections are being made. Sometimes it takes a train wreck to call attention to important issues. Satan 0- God 5

6) When Bryan re-awoke from the U.N. he had higher levels of awareness and increased mobility in extremities that had not had much movement before! For the first time he really moved his left arm and his left fingers were responding to commands! Satan 0 – God 6

7) Our faith in the sovereignty of God was raised to new heights. Our trust in faithful friends and total strangers (except for GRACE) was raised to new levels. Nothing quite like going into battle together to form deeper bonds. Satan 0 – God 7

8) Our immediate family: Hollie, Jen, and Isaiah (as well as Bryan's Uncle Jeff) were all able to be here for a critical day of testing. Because of the drama of the U.N. they had traveled quickly from Colorado and Indiana and would have otherwise missed this latest surgery and faith-test. There is no doubt they would have missed one of the most precious and intimate family prayer meetings in recorded family history had not God arranged otherwise. Satan 0 – God 8

9) BIGGER GOD! Most of our problems are not circumstantial, most of our problems are perceptual. Our biggest problem can be traced back to an inadequate understanding of who God is. Our problems seem really big because our God is really small. In fact, we reduce God to the size of our biggest problem. "A low view of God is the cause of a hundred lesser-evils, but a person with a high view of God is relieved of 10,000 temporal problems." A. W. Tozer. That's it — Our God had become BIGGER to us! Satan 0 – GOD 9

10) New appreciation for the concept of adoption. This thought was confirmed in a number of ways. Thank you all who made this thought come alive for us through your input. "Long before God laid the earth's foundation, He has us in mind. Long, long, ago He decided to adopt us into His family. He thought of everything, provided for everything we could possibly need." (Mark Batterson, pg. 29) Our God is all about adoption. Satan 0 – God 10

11) The final thought has been a common thread in so many of your emails and words to us. It has been the core of some of God's greatest works in my life: the theme of destiny! I believe my son will in the near future rise up from this temporary bed of affliction with a greater understanding of Destiny. He will walk in a faith much deeper than he has ever known as a result of this time in his life. All of this is an answer to the prayers of his Mom and Dad — but not quite how we expected it to happen. God rarely answers prayer quite the way we think he should. "For my thoughts are not your thoughts, neither are my ways your ways' declares the Lord." (Isaiah 55:8) Simply put — God's ways are much higher and much better than our ways. Satan 0 – God 11

This is my statement of faith, my defining moment of belief: I will trust God in the storms of my life as well as in the sunny days — because He is Trustworthy! I believe Satan is a loser! I believe that years ago in eternity past, Satan started a battle against God and God's children that he would stand no chance of winning. Christ has already won the victory and we're on the winning team!

Bryan, "When you find yourself in those challenging circumstances, you need to know that God is ordering your footsteps. You can have a sense of destiny because you know that God has considered every contingency in your life, and He always has your best interest at heart. And that sense of destiny, rooted in the sovereignty of God, helps you pray the unthinkable and attempt the impossible." (Mark Batterson, pg. 14)

May the God of all peace and comfort flood over each of your lives. Be encouraged our God lives and the battle belongs to the Lord. It is an HONOR to have such a great army of faith partners to carry us through our days here. Thank you!

Gratefully, Craig and Family

Chapter 20
THE STORM RAGES ON

As I contemplated the ending of the month of March, I was reminded of the old folklore saying I heard in grade school. March comes in like a lion and goes out like a lamb. Our March had come in like a pack of roaring lions. Would it go out peacefully? It was the last day of March. What a whirlwind of battles won! I was more than ready for March to be in the history books. I longed for a reprieve, but it was not to be.

As I returned to my son's bedside, I quickly realized that as a result of the loss of blood through hemorrhaging and surgery Bryan was continuing to receive blood transfusions. He should be feeling better. He should be gaining strength, yet he was not.

His body was at war again and his white blood cell count was climbing. His body was ravished with fever and chills. What was wrong?

As I again prayed to the God who heals, I felt drawn to check the packaged blood product Bryan was receiving through an intravenous line. I immediately pulled the emergency cord. Bryan was being transfused with the wrong blood type! They were giving him O+ blood. He was O negative. His already devastated body was fighting against the wrong life-giving blood he was receiving!

When the nurse came in, I informed her of the mistake. To her credit she immediately stopped the transfusion. In her alarm she consulted the chart an informed me that I was mistaken. The chart assured her he was indeed O positive. He had been typed and he was an O positive.

Why was everything so convoluted and mixed up?! Couldn't she just listen to me? I was his mother! I gave birth to him! I would not tell her something that was not true! I knew what his blood type was. It was on all his dog tags! Didn't they even check these critical things? Such were my thoughts.

Still it was up to me to prove his blood type. I went as quickly as I could back to my room to procure the dog tag he had given me before he left for Iraq. He was O negative.

As yet another investigation began it was clear what had happened. It was very troubling that the mistake had continued with every transfusion he had received from Day 1.

In the Battlefield O negative is always in short supply due to its rareness. Bryan needed massive amounts of this rare blood and the O negative they had in the field hospitals was being saved for females of childbearing age. The procedure to give O positive blood was born out of necessity and practicality on the battlefield.

Bryan's entire blood volume had been replaced and maintained by transfusions of O positive over the course of the previous month's injuries and surgeries.

In the future he would begin receiving his correct blood type and the symptoms of rejection, fever, chills and high white blood cell count should stop.

No doubt this had been a major cause of the fevers he had been fighting since his initial injuries.

Once again, I was shaken. I was also thankful that I was able to be with my son and follow the promptings of the spirit to check something that could have been fatal. If I had not been there, when would it have been discovered he was receiving the wrong blood type?

Incidents like this did not create in me a trusting attitude. I was constantly at attention praying unceasingly for my son's health and safety as I stood at his bedside watching every move. By Monday morning April 2, I reached out to our prayer warriors and expressed our son's need of prayer once again.

He was not doing well. His temperature was continuing to rise, and he had obvious intense pain in his private area. His lack of response to any verbal commands had become quite disconcerting also.

As we waited and prayed through the hours of suffering a song on the radio echoed closely our thoughts.

Praise you in This Storm (Casting Crowns)
I was sure by now
God, you would have reached down
And wiped our tears away
Stepped in and saved the day
But once again, I say "Amen" and it's still raining

As the thunder rolls
I barely hear your whisper through the rain
"I'm with you"
And as your mercy falls
I raise my hands and praise the The God who gives
And takes away

And I'll praise you in this storm
And I will lift my hands
For you are who you are
No matter where I am

And every tear I've cried
You hold in your hand
You never left my side
And though my heart is torn
I will praise you in this storm

I remember when I
I stumbled in the wind
You heard my cry to you
And raised me up again
My strength is almost gone

How can I carry on
If I can't find you

But as the thunder rolls
I barely hear your whisper through the rain
"I'm with you"
And as your mercy falls
I raise my hands and praise the God who gives
And takes away

And I'll praise you through this storm
And I will lift my hands
For you are who you are
No matter where I am

And every tear I've cried
You hold in your hand
You never left my side
And though my heart is torn
I will praise you in this storm

I will lift my eyes unto the hills
Where does my help come from?
My help comes from the Lord
The maker of Heaven and Earth

And I'll praise you in this storm
And I will lift my hands
For you are who you are
No matter where I am

And every tear I've cried
You hold in your hand
You never left my side
And though my heart is torn

I will praise you in this storm
Though my heart is torn
(Though my heart is torn)
I will praise you in this storm
(Praise you in this storm)

~Casting Crowns[4]

Tears of submission filled my eyes as I renewed my trust in a Sovereign God. Surely I had hoped that God would have stepped in and said "enough is enough! NO more!" But He had not. He did not.

I felt the pull of exhausted flesh and a broken heart to close my spirit to His gentle whisper that He was there with us, felt our sorrow and knew our confusion.

Everyday His mercy fell all around me. Though I was often blinded with tears by what my physical eyes could see, when I looked to where my true help came from my hope was restored and my resolve was established resolutely.

How many times had He indeed stepped in and saved the day? Too many to count! I would praise him in *this* storm.

Shortly after I had requested prayer, God sent one of his own warriors to Bryan's room for a divine appointment.

A Sergeant Major whom we had never met stopped by. He entered the room focused on one of his own.

We could tell immediately that he was a kindred spirit with ours and the Holy Spirit. Craig posted the following in the journal:

> There was no doubt what his purpose was. He was not there to make small talk, to talk military, to toot his horn. He was a man on a mission. He wanted to pray for Bryan and pray he did. With the unmistakable voice of a former drill Sgt, that raspy, rattling, deep, thundering almost cadence like tone, he began to pray. To say that the gates of hell were shaken would be an understatement. He didn't care who heard him, three rooms away, or what rank they were. There was not a politically correct bone in his body. He prayed over Bryan as if he was his own son, He cried out to Father God to heal Bryan and to raise him up to glorify him. He informed Satan, that NO weapon formed against him would work, that he was God's kid. He repeatedly spoke truth over Bryan. He spoke in faith believing that God was going to fully restore him to total and complete health.

Craig and I fell completely in agreement with him. We were ministered to in the deepest longings of our heart for our son. After gathering me in his muscled arms he was gone as quickly as he had come.

The presence of God remained heavy in the room. Our eyes filled with tears of thankfulness for God's tender mercies evident by display of mercy shown us by a complete stranger known only to God himself.

It became apparent within a few short hours that our son was again struggling for his life. As they wheeled him back to emergency surgery, we clung to the truth proclaimed over our son by our unknown but dearly loved Sergeant Major.

That night after Bryan's surgery Craig wrote the following in the Caring bridge journal:

Our dear Marine/boy has undergone yet another emergency surgery in his very sensitive area. To say this area has been the target of Satan repeated times in this journey would be understating the facts. The destroyer is "hell bent" on destroying our son and his future. The surgeon called back and told us we had caught it just in time.

I believe that Satan is a defeated enemy, but he doesn't know it yet. I believe God is Everything His word declares Him to be and so much more. I believe that He has all power in heaven and earth. I believe that He is the ultimate healer and the Giver of Life. I believe that He came to give us abundant Life, here and now. I believe He is Bigger than any of our problems and challenges of life. I believe He is the Everlasting God, the Bright and Morning Star. I believe He commands an Army, the likes this world has never seen. I believe that one day all mankind will answer to, "What have you done with my Son Jesus?" I believe that one day very soon, the Ancient of days will step back into this thing we call time and right every wrong and Holy Justice will fall on this earth. I believe this same

God desires a relationship with us more than we will ever know. I believe that He is ready to do far more in our lives, if we would only Believe HIM. Do you Believe God is who He says He is??

Thanks for hearing my heart. I just had to get that off my chest.

How Great THOU Art,
Bryan's dad

Chapter 21
FINAL DAYS

Days melted into nights that became bonus days to believe God for the new mercies He promised every fresh morning. It is true that our physical bodies were exhausted, our minds muddled at times, but the inexplicable peace that God gave clung to us like the dew on the fresh green sprouts of grass that pushed aside the winter's covering of spent leaves outside our window. Hope was one of the greatest gifts offered us through the turbulent days still to come. For it was Hope that would recover what the enemy of our souls had relentlessly pursued. In each offering of prayer, homemade meal delivered, bedside visit, flowers sent, resources offered, Hope, faith, love, peace, and kindness were showered on us by the body of Christ throughout our stay at The National Navy Medical Center in Bethesda, Maryland. Prayers arose around the world for our beloved son. We continued to be amazed at what the Spirit of the living God did in the hearts and lives of a growing group of believers who would band together to pray for another's son.

Still the assaults continued in procession on Bryan's health like the routine movement of the hands on a clock. These were very troubling occurrences as they threatened his very life.

On this particular day they failed to come get me after what had become a routine wash-out surgery for them. It was never routine for us. We had been witnesses to unbelievable missteps too many times.

After being overly patient, I set off to find my missing son who had been pushed aside behind a curtain in the large, darkened surgery theatre room. He was awake, arms tied down and positioned flat on his back. He was crying silently in terror, fighting to sit up as he choked on vomit pooled in his throat, clogging his trache. I quickly untied him and held him up in my arms as I cried into the room where compassion had left him alone.

"How does this happen? I cried out to the God Who Sees everything. "Why does this happen?" I sobbed aloud.

Another investigation ensued. Craig and I were brought in. Apologies were made. It would never happen again.

Yet it did. It was the day Virginia Tech was on lock-down engulfed in unimaginable horror. We were in the waiting room. A corpsman was to come get me before they brought Bryan back to his room. Once again, I felt compelled to go back to his room early. Hollie went with me. Bryan had just returned from the OR, but they had failed to notify me. He was tied down prone on his back fighting against the restraints to sit up.

Again, the vomit had pooled in his throat and he could do nothing about it. Hot angry tears fled his panicked eyes as vomit flowed down the sides of his face into his ears. It was oozing and bubbling out of the trache in his neck. He was drowning! He had asphyxiated it into his damaged lungs.

He would develop pneumonia in both lungs as a result. Springing into action we untied his restraints and raised him up as the full force of his blockage came forth.

I was as furious as any mother would have been. I pulled the emergency cord and rushed out of the room calling for help. Leaving Hollie to attend to Bryan I marched down to the Marine Corp Liaison office on the fifth floor and took out the full force of a mother's rage on all present.

This would NEVER happen again! They would assure by whatever means they could that Bryan would never be left ALONE again! How could this keep happening over and over to one of their own??

After yet another investigation it was decided that Bryan would now have his own personal corpsman that would stay by his side. Always. Further I would be allowed to sit directly outside his operating room and be with him in the recovery room. This was done to try to gain back our trust in a system that had repeatedly failed our son and us as a family. Hollie wrote an entry in our Caringbridge journal.

Dearest Family (consider yourself adopted!)

As I was reading through all your prayers and messages to us and Bryan these past few days, my heart was so full of thanksgiving and love for you. After a "good cry" I wanted to tell you thank you! Your prayers, encouragement, love support, faithfulness, hope, joy, strength, and concern mean more to us than we could ever hope to express. May our Father, who never slumbers or sleeps, honor you for your steadfast belief in HIM who is able to heal and restore. He is our HOPE, our strong Tower, and our very great reward! Bryan was with us again today, both physically and mentally. His care has MUCH improved and he got a shave, Old Spice cologne, and new break-away boxers to go around his fixation. He looked like a new man. Last night he was playing catch with one of the corpsmen and then she had him giving her the trekkie hand symbol — too funny! He hasn't said too much, in fact the other night that Mom mentioned (when he reached up and hugged her) was the last time he has spoken. Please pray for that. We know that it's not because he can't, but we all feel that Bryan is very sad. I am sure he and God have some stuff that they are sorting out together in his mind. Pray that Bryan remembers how much God loves him and how to right every wrong and to bring such beauty from such despair. What a trade off!

I will be on the midnight watch with Bryan tonight and I consider all these weeks by his bed an honor and a privilege. As many of you know personally, Bryan is an exceptional person. A true friend and a joy to be around. He is a pretty sensitive guy (growing up with two sisters will do that to a person) and he has been emotionally shaken these last few days. We are getting sweet hugs, face pats, and many tears from him. Continue to pray for Bryan's heart, that God would not let any bitterness take root and that God would give Bryan a heart like HIS.

I have told my parents before, and they are probably due another telling. I have received from them the greatest heritage a parent can give their child- a godly legacy, a spiritual inheritance that is priceless to me. Mom used to pray for all of us kids years back this particular verse. It has been floating around in my mind for Bryan these last few weeks (the last part is what she prayed for us) — Isaiah 61:2-3 (NIV) "to proclaim the year of the LORD's favor and the day of vengeance of our God, to comfort all who mourn, and provide for those who grieve in Zion — to bestow on them a crown of beauty instead of ashes, the oil of gladness instead of mourning, and a garment of praise instead of a spirit of despair. THEY WILL BE CALLED OAKS OF RIGHTEOUSNESS, A PLANTING OF THE LORD FOR THE DISPLAY OF HIS SPLENDOR." (emphasis mine) How beautifully God is turning Bryan's life into a display of HIS splendor- praise Him. Thank you, Mom and Dad.

Thank YOU dear, dear extended family — may you feel a part of ours and know the great, deep, and matchless love of our Father's heart toward you! Be richly blessed

Every night around 11:00 p.m. I would be instructed by Craig and Hollie to go back to the room and take my pills and go to sleep. It was very frustrating and humbling to be sent to bed like a child when I wanted so badly to stay. With tears in my eyes, I would set off into the darkness to locate the car I had parked hours before under the troubling effects of sleeping pills. Often, I would call out in whispered prayers for help finding my elusive car.

Always I would find my way aided by unseen hands or oftentimes by a kind stranger. The pills took effect quickly and consciousness left me for at least 8 hours. After that I could function but often had trouble remembering the details of my early morning routine after I had completed them.

By leaving at 11:00 p.m., I had 9 hours to find the car, drive to the hotel, sleep, bathe, dress and drive back to the hospital. Finding a place to park and making my way through the confusing maze that separated me from my son left no time for breakfast.

Relieving my husband was always a bitter-sweet time. It was so good to see him, and I was sad to see him go. He would give me a brief rundown on the night and be gone in minutes anxious for time away.

He was not as desperate for sleep as before. Bryan's new room on the fifth floor had an extra bed in it and it had one chair. It was a somber reality that despite the presence of a corpsman we still could not trust Bryan's care without constant family supervision. We had come in from lunch more than once to find the corpsman sleeping on the job. One time he left never to be found that day. We discontinued the use of the corpsman as it clearly wasn't effective.

Our days were full of activity the likes we had never seen before. It had the intensity of a mash unit with constant life and death issues. We quickly learned how to recognize his needs and to make sure they were addressed. We came to observe which nurses and corpsmen were passionate about their jobs and those who long ago lost compassion for their brother and were simply doing a chore. We watched his meds and Craig became an expert with the I.V. equipment, managing the beeps and alarms that consistently rang out. He was excellent with the visitors that came in a never- ending stream. He was the one who sat with Bryan night after night praying for him ready to embrace him if he should ever awake. Hollie was excellent with her brother and was instantly at his side if ever he showed signs of alertness. She understood him when he talked around his trache and was there to encourage him when the truth was hard to receive. She helped us take care of him. Her help was priceless. We could never have made it through those terrorizing first months without her.

Craig wrote the following on the evening of April 6th. It was Good Friday.

Good evening son,

As I sit here in your room with you tonight, I praise God for technology. We are now able to get internet access in your room. What a day you have had. I hardly know where to begin, it seems every few hours is critical and your condition changes so quickly. Overall today you were pretty rested and sorta pain free. You had some problems with the ol' Foley catheter. You did sit up in a wheelchair for nearly 2 hrs. today. You weren't exactly wide awake, but you held your head high anyway. You are still gaining strength, but the reality is that a lot of the time you are operating at the level of a 2-3 year-old. I just want you to know the whole truth and no sugar coating. Months or even years later when you read this journal of faith you will know just how far God has really brought you. None of us believe that you are going to stay at this level, but today, it's where you are at.

You are playing catch with your stress ball and throwing it at whoever will catch it. You will talk with us about every 3rd day. Not sure what's up with that. We are so excited every time you bless us with words. Your whole body has undergone so much trauma and shock, it's a wonder you are alive. You are moving your entire body around, all over the bed, pulling yourself up and exercising your legs. The nurses you've had the last few days have been amazing. Robyn and Gabriel are truly angels sent here by God. They both seem to have a genuine faith in your Everlasting God. And yes of course they have heard your song. We sense that you are getting pretty weak and frankly just sick and tired of being flat on your back in this hospital.

You had another busy day of visitors today. The assistant Commandant of the Marine Corp came in with his wife. The Secretary of State Condoleezza Rice came in to see you. Some pretty cool people, all here to thank you for your sacrifice and service to this country we call home. More and more each night you are getting longer and longer periods of rest. The main issue is your infections. They are being treated heavily. In your most recent wrestling match with three strong people, somehow you managed to pull out your feeding tube for the third time. The only thing worse than pulling it out is putting it back in. I have watched them do it 2 times and it is not pleasant. We look forward each day to your consistent improvement. It appears you will not be going to the OR anytime soon, so with no setbacks via surgeries, we expect you to really make some gigantic leaps forward in the near future.

Bottom line — you are truly one very brave and strong Marine. You have endured so many painful issues over the past weeks. Your God is developing a man of God that He can really use greatly.

Unfortunately, we recognize suffering as one of his methods/tools to do that. He is always more concerned about our character than He is our comfort. We pray daily that you will not become angry at Him for all you have gone through. Your heavenly Father loves you so very much and is really concerned about your walk with Him. You are going to have to trust us ol grey heads on this one, God is on your side despite what your circumstances are telling you.

You should also know that your story is growing to over 16,000 people who have read about your amazing story of God's deliverance in your life. That story is getting larger in our eyes. We are beginning to hear from your unit. From those who were eyewitnesses to the IED blast. They said it was so big that it left a huge crater in the road. It took your 13-ton vehicle and spun it around like it was one of your Tonka trucks from days gone by. We never knew when you were playing in the sand box, back in rural Indiana, that one day you would be in a much bigger sandbox called Iraq. Your bravery continues to amaze and inspire all who read about it. Once again, I tell you, as your father, how very proud I am of you I am. Your courage and bravery must come from somewhere else, because I do know that it did not come from your dad.

Hebrews 11:1 ~ Faith means being sure of the things we hope for and knowing that something is real, even if we do not see it, Faith is the reason we remember great people who have lived in the past. This has been one of those faith building moments in your LIFE that will be life altering.
Love your dad

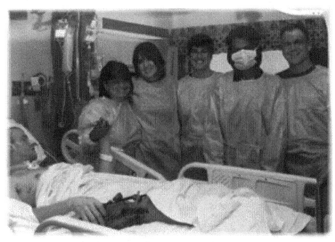

Pam (friend), Hollie, Granda,
Condoleeza Rice (Secretary of State, and Craig

In the stillness of night Hollie journaled the following:

Hello family,

I am very happy to report that Bryan had a peaceful night. He got the silly feeding tube put back in, ouch! He has had darn bad luck with those things. And after his meds he settled down and went to sleep. Poor guy, he had flat worn himself out! We are so thankful for his rest, it is one of our top prayers, rest means his body is more or less pain free and it can continue the healing process. Keep praying for rest and NO pain — the doctors are constantly doing the balancing act between too sleepy from the meds to wake up or in too much pain. Pray that the Maker and Creator of Bryan's body would give them some tips on His patient.

Bryan is getting pretty thin. He has been here for a long time now and his body has had to undergo so much trauma. He bulked up in Iraq and it was a good thing as his body has needed that extra weight and muscle, he is strong still but thin. He is being fed through the feeding tube, but the tube is positioned below his stomach, so we are told that he always feels hungry. How sad! Pray that the Bread of Life would sustain him and give him energy, strength, and fullness.

Bryan hasn't been awake enough these last few days to do more than give a few hugs and touch our faces as we stand beside his bedside. These moments are precious, and we are anxious for the days when his body has bounced back enough for him to talk and stay alert with us. His alertness and responsiveness to the doctors and the physical therapists is important for his rehab so pray that he would be awake and alert when he needs to be and resting comfortably the rest of the time. We know that whereas we are physically standing by his bed there are countless more of you all standing with Bryan in prayer all over the US and the world — thank you, thank you!

Have a great Easter weekend. We serve a Risen, ALIVE, Active, Powerful, Death Conquering Savior! He has taken away our sin, our death, and offers us LIFE abundantly in exchange- how just like a loving Father, He has taken our place instead. Praise Him, our Risen Lord! Blessed Easter! With all Love and Thanks,
Hollie Chambers

On Easter Morning Craig and Hollie slipped away to attend church services at the church she attended when she went to American University. I was kept company by the presence of a Navy Chaplain that we had become well acquainted with. It was a quiet morning. Bryan continued to be unresponsive as we waited to see what God would do on this celebrated day in the lives of all believers. Later that evening Craig wrote the following in Bryan's journal:

Wow Bryan,

You have given us an unforgettable Easter. Actually, God is the one who has outdone himself, again, on our behalf. I hardly know where to begin to tell you all that has transpired on this unforgettable Easter Sunday. Hollie and I went to her old church, National Community Church, or the "theatre church". To say that the Risen

Lord was present there would be an understatement of the fact. Some of you who have been following this story for awhile will recognize the name Mark Batterson. He is the pastor of this church and the author of the book "In a Pit with a Lion on a Snowy Day." I cannot begin to tell you how powerful that book has ministered to me as I stood by your bedside, night after night. Well of course I happened to have that book with me when I went to NCC. God ordained a divine appointed meeting with Mark and yes, he signed my book. The service felt tailor-made for the Chambers family, from the first song to the last. Amen. God is so good to his hurting kids who just can't seem to get enough of Him. Rather out of character for this cutting- edge church, the worship team decided to do one of the "old hymns." One I knew quite well but was not prepared for the line out of the 2nd verse, which leaped from the screen. The song "He Lives" was well suited for an Easter service, and no doubt many of you may have sung it today. The line out of the 2nd verse, "I know that He is leading through all the STORMY BLAST", was one that God seem to speak directly to my soul. You see Bryan, on February 28, you encountered a "stormy Blast of huge proportions. One that made a bid for your very life, But God. The same God who tells the oceans were to stop. Who tells the sun when to shine, and placed all the mountains in their exact locations, told this IED how much damage it could do to you. The Everlasting God has spared you from death.

Praise His HOLY name!!

But your story keeps getting better. Today at about 3 p.m., God decided to do some restoration and resurrection work in YOUR life. We got the OK to give you some ice chips. Well it seems to have really woke you up. Then a Marine friend Patrick showed up with the founder of "Operation Second Chance" Cindy ?, who came bearing gifts from afar. Quite amazing gifts actually. A portable play station, a portable DVD player, 2 movies, a game, and a memory card. For the first time in a long time you awoke and gave her the Biggest Smile we have seen. You decided while you were at it to go ahead and speak and to tell her thanks for all of it. At which point your mom who was watching this miracle of re-awakening unfold before her very eyes, began to cry with joy. There was not a dry eye in the room, the chaplain was there as well.

The plan for this week is: The Big 3 — Get rid of the trachea, the feeding tube, and the foley catheter. Almost all of those hinge on your passing the speech/swallow test. So, we are asking all to pray that you pass with flying colors. Your prayer partners are growing and their part in this amazing Easter, will never go unnoticed by this humble and grateful family here in the shadow of our Nation's Capital.

Pastor Mark closed with this timely and awesome verse out of Jude 1:24-25,

"To Him who is able to keep you from falling and to present you before His glorious presence without fault and with great joy — to the only God our Savior be glory, majesty, power, and authority through Jesus Christ our Lord, before all ages, now and forevermore! Amen!"
Your amazed and full of faith,
Father

Chapter 22
UNDER THE
COVER OF DARKNESS

The days immediately following Easter were abounding in giant steps forward as our Everlasting God made His healing of our son evident. Within days Bryan had his trache removed and he had passed his swallow test. With delight we watched him take his first drink of a McDonald's milkshake and feast upon a popsicle. He had lost over a hundred pounds and was little more than a skeleton wrapped in flesh.

Just as quickly his catheter was gone, and he was learning to use the bathroom again. Gradually he spent more time sitting up in his bedside chair till it was time for Physical Therapy to start working with him to develop strength in muscles that had wasted away.

During these long and painful days our son seldom talked and was very troubled in spirit. In a rare emotional outburst, he spoke of suicide and our hearts broke anew at the depth of his emotional agony as he struggled to face a life he despaired of living. The emotional weight of losing a limb exceeded the physical weight and pain he felt as his external fixator hit the walker with every hop he made. Still with grit and determination, he gave all he had to propel himself forward.

He continued to battle with infections, surgeries and the agonizingly painful beginnings of flashbacks associated with the IED blast. Additional painful recollections intertwined in his injured memory brought sorrow.

In more private settings, times of pain were accompanied by counting out loud. Bryan would start counting at ten and continue to one hundred ninety-nine. His worried frustrated desire was to count higher, but he could not, so he would start from the beginning in mechanical repetition over and over. It became very obvious that Bryan's Traumatic Brain Injury would need specialized therapy. He was receiving none at Bethesda.

In the midst of ongoing investigations into the medical mishaps that had occurred in Bryan's care we began to hear recommendations directing us to a VA hospital in Tampa, Florida. We were encouraged to consider this cutting-edge facility. It had a polytrauma unit that could address Bryan's multiple traumatic injuries with personalized expertise. The recommendation implied that the facility had a proven record. We were told there was no longer anything else the National Navy Medical Center could do for our son. Moving would be his best choice.

We were assured that the transfer of our son would occur over the next several weeks and would be accompanied by several preparatory video conferences in the meantime. These conferences were to introduce us to the team of doctors who would be intimately involved with Bryan's continued recovery. We were assured that they would know everything they possibly could about him and his injuries. They would be well acquainted with his preferences and stock the pantry with all his favorite foods. It would be the ultimate place of healing for our son. There he would receive the therapy for his traumatic brain injury that he was desperately in need of.

The move would not take place until all parties were assured that this was the best place for Bryan. It was under this understanding that we signed the request to have our son transferred. We were hopeful that this place of new beginnings would be just what Bryan and our family needed. We had great expectations of the weeks to come. It couldn't hurt to be in sunny Florida either!

We started making the mental move from the place we had come to all those weeks ago. We had been walking these sacred halls for fifty-two life altering days. Our hearts had embraced many people that had become so dear to us. Some were families that had a son, a husband, a father that had suffered alongside our son.

Many were the doctors and nurses we had come to love and appreciate. I found comfort in the presence of the chaplain who spent many hours with me at Easter and the Friar that stood in the distance approaching only when our eyes would meet. Quickly, silently he would slip a small card with an image of Christ upon it into my hand and just as quickly back out of the room and be gone having never said a word.

Then there were the special people who spent their off days standing with me and personally entering the valley of the shadow of war. It was easy to count them as cherished blessings. We could count them one by one.

God himself was our greatest blessing. He had been so faithful. We had witnessed so many undeniable miracles. We had been embraced by local churches and the amazing people that came to offer support. He had surrounded us with many fellow followers of the Gospel of Christ in the halls of the President's hospital. They had been His hands and feet. We were deeply humbled. We had been upheld by the Body of Christ across the world by the outpouring of unnumbered prayers. Our room was full of tangible, thoughtful gifts of all kinds, delicious home prepared meals stocked the refrigerator, bath products overflowed the limited space in the shower, flowers scented the air, books filled the bedside stand, music waited to be heard and a beautiful handcrafted quilt covered me during the darkest of nights. We felt loved and we would miss everyone greatly.

As I lay my head down on that April 24 evening, I was thankful that we would have some days to say our goodbyes. We would need everyone.

The following morning, I awoke as normal and made my way to Bryan's bedside. When I arrived I found Bryan's room empty. His bed had been stripped leaving only a lone pillow entwined in his rumpled sheet. All his personal effects were gone. Craig and Bryan were nowhere to be seen. I stood motionless in the center of the room trying to make sense of the emptiness.

It was a busy morning for as usual I always came just after shift change. I received blank looks when I inquired about Bryan's whereabouts at the nurse's station. The nurse followed me to Bryan's room to assess the odd situation. Maybe he had been moved to another room? No one knew where he was.

Bewildered I went to the Marine Corps Liaison office. Parker followed me back to Bryan's empty room. As he stood in the doorway, I saw unbelief etched on his face. Unbelief that transformed into a well restrained internal anger.

It would appear that Bryan had been transported by medivac under the cover of night and no one had been told. Bryan and Craig were on their way to Tampa, Florida. I was stunned! We were told we would have video conferences where we would have time to be assured of our decision to transition. I was not ready. I needed time to transition. Time had evaporated. We would have no time. None.

It became clear that someone of higher authority wanted us gone. The quicker the better. Journalists were always poking around looking for a story. The National Navy Medical Center had been the subject of too many articles that spring.

In tears I returned to Bryan's hospital room where we had experienced so much joy and unrestrained sorrow. Even then in the characteristic emptiness of a stripped-down hospital room I felt the lingering presence of our Everlasting God our strong deliverer. Taking a few moments of remembrance, I buried my face in Bryan's lone pillow and emptied muffled sobs and prayers of thankfulness amid shock.

I hurried back to our room at the Navy Lodge to awaken Hollie. Together we quickly logged on the Caringbridge site to read Craig's last entry he wrote shortly after midnight.

Bon voyage to Bethesda Naval Hospital
To my only son,

Good evening Bryan, buddy. You had better get some good rest tonight. Moments ago, they came in and said that at 0600 we will get on our medevac flight and fly to Tampa. How exciting is that!!! Great God news is how I am looking at it. As I set here in this hospital room and reflect on the past 51 days here, I have to say I get a big lump in my throat. Where is that coming from???

I do know it's not sadness, but Joy! How much can one little family endure in 51 days?? I can tell you this, a lot more than any of us could ever have thought. Yet in comparison we have endured so little. You cannot see all of what we have seen around here. You are oblivious to the levels of pain and suffering that has been all around us here. Our fellow comrades in ICU have endured so much more than we could ever imagine. Some of them like DJ's mom, are still there going on 75 days in ICU. DJ, a fellow Marine, is fighting for his life every day.

I remember vividly our final days in ICU. I met a retired Navy Admiral and his sweet family. They were there with his dear wife of 57 years, battling a host of life-threatening issues. I was quite drawn to the stately old gentleman. We struck up one of those friendships without the formality of names. I had the privilege of getting to know a little of their history together, only to find out that she was born and raised in Crawfordsville, Indiana. They met there and married there. He even attended a year at Wabash College. Small world and getting smaller. You see Crawfordsville is only about 30 miles from where I grew up. Long story short, I noticed one morning that all the doctors and family had a closed-door session. Later that morning I came back to the waiting room to find him sitting there alone. I sat down and he told me that he could not stand to be in the room with his 3 precious daughters as they told their mother goodbye and removed her from life support. I was able to pray with him and for him and attempt in some small way to help him through this hard time of life. We both cried, and I said good-bye to a sweet, short time friend. I will look him up on the other side of Eternity. Bryan, you are probably wondering what that has to do with you?? Only to say that all around you/us is suffering and pain. The world is full of it.

It seems we were a little closer to it after spending 51 days here. To conclude, there are guys here better off than you and some worse off than you. God has been gracious to you through it all. We are humbled by His mercy to us.

Hollie reiterated in a recent posting how far God has brought you. You see we were told that we could be flying in to Bethesda to tell you good-bye. But God had other plans for you.

So many of those writing to you have referenced the verse in Jeremiah, "I know the plans I have for you, plans to prosper you, plans to give you a future and a hope." God's hope and commitment to you is truly incredible. He loves us so much and will not let us remain where we are at.

I leave you with this amazing quote from the Bible.

1 Corinthians "Blessed be the Father of our Lord Jesus Christ, the father of mercies and the God of all comfort, who comforts us in all our tribulation, that we may be able to comfort those who are in any trouble, with the comfort with which we ourselves are comforted by God."

So that is the deal here Bryan, God expects us to deal with others with His comfort and message of HOPE.

Thanks again to all of you prayer warriors and partners for being on board with us and being such an incredible encouragement to this family.

Sincerely, Craig, Granda, Hollie, Jenn

Once again, I chose to encourage my heart in the truth of what my husband wrote and took my cue from him. Even though I had misgivings and needed the transition time to say goodbye, I would go forward with hope for the days ahead. Quickly we packed every square inch of the Buick with all we could possibly fit inside. We gifted many of the precious offerings we had to leave behind to two very grateful housekeepers.

After spending hours getting copies of all of Bryan's medical records, including an astounding amount of all his medications, we slipped out the guarded gates for the last time.

Leaving the campus of the National Naval Medical Center for the long drive to Tampa, we looked forward with great expectation to the opportunities that lay ahead for Bryan at the famed VA in sunny Florida.

Chapter 23
40 DAYS AND NIGHTS

Around 8:00 p.m. only a few hours into our journey to Tampa, we received an impassioned call from Craig. They had arrived at the VA after an exceptionally long day of pickups and deliveries. Bryan had been the last delivery. He had hung suspended in his gurney for over 12 hours on the C-130.

Our Marine had fared well on the journey, but he had not received any of his meds since he had left Bethesda. Bryan's pain level was steadily climbing and still Craig hadn't been able to persuade the VA to administer any of his meds. He was informed that a mix-up had occurred, and it would take time to straighten everything out. Craig was desperate for us to get there with Bryan's pain medications. We drove with haste.

When we arrived from our 900-mile journey to Tampa, we went straight to the VA with Bryan's meds. Once there we were dismayed to find that despite the intense pain he was experiencing, the VA would not allow him to take any of the medications we had brought with us! Our son had been without his scheduled medications for over 30 hours with no pain relief available in the foreseeable future.

Rejecting Bryan's medical records from Bethesda, it had been decided that Bryan would need to be seen by doctors and have blood work and x-rays done at their facility. Once these procedures were done Bryan would then, and only then, receive medications prescribed by the VA.

Our son was delirious with pain. Craig was exhausted having been up for over 36 hours, and Hollie and I were both tired and emotionally spent from our 900-mile journey from Washington, D.C.

It was a disastrous start for the newest chapter in Bryan's journey at the James A. Haley VA in Tampa, Florida. We had been oversold. In fact, nothing we had been told had its basis in any of our reality. Not only did The James A. Haley VA NOT know everything there was to know about our son as promised, they didn't even have a room for him in the Polytrauma wing. A partially cleaned out tiny broom closet became his new home. It became increasingly clear that the VA was as surprised at our arrival as we were of our departure from Bethesda.

We were deeply saddened to realize that we had been manipulated by the office of the Public Relations and our healthcare mediator at Bethesda. It would appear our son had been recommended to the VA only to remove him from the controversy surrounding the many investigations at Bethesda. Those with power were not going to allow Bryan to stay a day longer than necessary once we signed the permission for transfer. We felt painfully deceived. The move was not about what was best for Lance Corporal Bryan Chambers, rather it appeared to be about what was best for The National Navy Medical Center's public relations.

Again, we had entered into a new culture where we were severely lacking skills to navigate the existing system. In Bethesda we had been assigned our Marine officer, Parker, to help us navigate the Department of Defense. Here we had no one. Unknown to us novices we had come under the guidelines of the Veterans Administration which was operating under a completely different set of rules and policies. We were reeling from the trauma of the intense days behind us in Bethesda and ill prepared to take on the challenges the VA would present us with. Nothing was as promised in the glowing sales job that had been presented.

The James A. Haley VA Polytrauma Unit was simply a small wing in a typical VA hospital were the veterans were much older than our son. It felt more like a nursing home than a cutting-edge hospital.

We were grateful for the increase in prayer support we had on Bryan's Caringbridge site, but we were deeply frustrated that we had left behind the tangible support system Bryan and our family had developed in Washington, D.C.

We chose to cry out to God for His strength and for desire to give this new place a chance. In truth we wanted nothing more than to pack our bags and leave.

While Bryan continued to heal in fits and starts it was not because of any special treatment he received in Tampa. God was using time and interaction with us, his family to return him to his memory.

It grieves me to give a bad report of the majority of the nursing staff at the Polytrauma Unit at James A. Haley VA in Tampa. I can only pray that what we experienced at that time was an anomaly. With the exception of a nurse named Bill, who was a retired Marine and one female nurse, they did not treat our war torn Marine with the care, respect and honor he deserved. They were decidedly uncaring and unhelpful. It was disheartening and overwhelming for our family.

He had been there for 10 days before he got his first bedside bath and he developed sepsis in his pin site wounds from lack of care. The nurses themselves didn't appear to realize that they worked in a unit renown for brain trauma. In fact, they gave the impression that they had not been educated about traumatic brain injury at all and certainly not the ensuing symptoms! They were vocal about how personally offended they were when those symptoms presented themselves in Bryan's healing process.

Bryan continued to be very sick physically and ended up back in the ICU for a few days. In addition, his severe brain injury presented itself with little to no short-term memory. It was a very alarming and devastating injury to our son. The symptoms presented themselves in ways that shook our emotions and broke our hearts. He experienced hallucinations and he was deeply afraid. He had the mentality of a toddler and it was beyond excuse for him to be mistreated and neglected by the nursing staff.

Some staff members went so far as to argue with him and raise their voices. Shamefully, some who named the name of Christ refused to be his nurse when assigned to him for their shift. It was disgraceful. They should have been fired, but their behavior was not only tolerated but excused. They gossiped about us as a family further alienating us from support groups or new faces that might have been a source of help and comfort. I had to advocate every single day for the care he needed as if he was the unwanted stepchild on the polytrauma wing.

Despite the turmoil we encountered at the VA, God redeemed our experience in Tampa by ministering to us in exceptionally intimate ways. We met many caring people of faith at Idlewild Baptist Church. These exceptional individuals reached out to us in our time of distress and became personally invested in our lives as the stress of continued trauma revealed the beginnings of painful fractures in our close-knit family relationships. During those 40 trying days they took time out of their lives to bless us with friendship, counsel and support.

Despite the hardships that threatened to destroy our family in Tampa, it was in this place God chose to bring our son back to his memory.

Bryan had become very adept at shutting the doctors and therapists out. He simply pulled the sheet over his head when he was done participating.

One particular night, May 31, to be exact, Craig decided to keep Bryan up longer than normal and not allow him to go to bed. Craig was determined to find a certain courtyard on the grounds to which we had never been. In his God given wisdom, he knew we needed privacy and had heard that this garden was a rarely discovered and beautifully peaceful place. As Craig wheeled Bryan in his borrowed wheelchair our son expressed his strong desire to go back to his room immediately. He wanted to go to bed and use his sheet as a shield against the never-ending day. He was done. So done.

Craig refused.

To say that Craig's firm denial brought out the worst in our son would be an understatement. As his mother I was greatly distressed at his violent behavior. I pleaded to abort the outing. I wanted to return this foul-mouthed stranger masquerading in my son's broken body back to his room and flee. With steely perseverance Craig pressed on.

Bryan burst the quiet solitude of the beautiful courtyard with wave upon wave of pent up rage, confusion and sorrow. When finally broken by grief, he allowed reality to confront his deepest denial. With uncontrolled sobs he verbally confessed his fearful reality. It was NOT just a nightmare that sleep would take away!

"I thought I was in a really, really bad dream!" he sobbed. "I thought if I could ONLY go to sleep, I would wake up and NONE of this would be real! I thought I was DREAMING!! Dad am I not dreaming?!" He pleaded. "Oh God I am not DREAMING??!!"

With sobs of desperation his ghastly reality shook him from the clutches of the coma that had held him and his full senses prisoner for three months.

Craig cried aloud to the unseen God Who Sees to come quickly to our aid. We wept openly with turbulent emotion as we watched our son bear sorrow too heavy for him to hold inside. He voiced sorrow upon sorrow as he struggled with spoken memory of war's mental and physical wounds. The four of us wept and agonized our grim hellish reality for long minutes barely able to breath.

"Jesus!" I cried internally, "There has to be another way! Please take this sorrow away! Please Jesus!"

Talking over the top of each other we attempted to answer his tormenting questions only to be caught in another wave of shared grief.

As the colossal waves slowly subsided to gradual ripples of painful acceptance of our reality, I became aware of a solitary figure sitting directly across from us in the covering of the lengthening shadows. Tears dripped down his wrinkled face as he acknowledged without sound that he had heard and felt every sacred painful word shouted, sobbed and spoken.

It was the most horribly treasured outing we had ever taken together. We had interrupted that beautiful peaceful courtyard garden with a raging stranger, but we left with our precious son who had been painfully liberated by an act of God. We each retreated from the garden changed by our own type of Gethsemane experience. We submitted to God's sovereign will for a future that we could not see. Peacefulness in the garden was restored.

Chapter 24
WALTER REED

That very evening became the beginning of the end of our stay in Tampa Florida. In four, amazingly-God-choreographed days that included an unforgettable overnight stay at a beautiful beach house on Anna Maria Island, Bryan and Craig would again be boarding a C-130 and flying back to our nation's capital.

Hollie and I would bring up the rear. She in the car and I on a commercial airline. This time our destination was The Walter Reed Army Medical Center in D.C.

Walter Reed was known for its advances in prosthetics and Bryan's leg was in need of focused attention as it still failed to heal properly.

Once again, we entered a military system that propelled us into the unknown. This was not so obvious when I attended the orientation for all new patients and their families to the medical center. Filled with hope and equipped with a days-worth of knowledge from the orientation along with pages of information about procedures and caseworkers, I was directed to find a table marked with the letter C after Bryan's last name, Chambers.

Imagine my consternation when those manning the table could find no record of a Bryan Chambers. In those next few minutes I received an education that would mark the rest of our stay at Walter Reed. Walter Reed was an Army hospital. Bryan was a Marine.

It would appear that the two branches did not relate to each other at ALL. Each had separate ways and procedures that in no way overlapped. I had the feeling they barely tolerated each other. Nothing I had internalized that day applied to Marines. I had wasted my time and Bryan and I were relegated to the position of a square peg in a round hole. We just didn't fit in. The Army and the Marine Corps were polarized.

I was directed to a small office that you found only when you were hopelessly lost. It was far away in the dark recesses of the sprawling army base. Once found the office was hidden in what seemed to be an old discarded coach's office of bygone years. The surrounding gym and rooms had the appearance of being shuttered for decades. The makeshift office was manned by a very small group of injured Marines put in charge of answering questions for which they did not have the answers. It was the equivalent of a cardboard prop office. In name only. There I received little information about procedures and was left for the remaining months to do the best I could to find my own solutions. It was up to me to educate myself on ways to make sure my son received the treatment he was entitled to. In reality Bryan should have been recommended, and we should have requested to go back to the National Naval Medical Center in Bethesda where Marines were treated. In our naivety we didn't realize it was an option as we had been told in April that there was nothing else that could be done for Bryan there.

The months ahead were made incredibly more difficult as a result of living at an army base. Bryan was placed in the amputee Ward 57 in the hospital for an additional ten days where he underwent additional surgeries to streamline his external fixation on his right leg.

It was at this time it became clear that it was possible Bryan's leg might not heal enough to receive the internal nail meant to help it mend. Being fitted for a prosthetic would have to be postponed till healing occurred in his femur.

In the waiting period his means of transportation was an oversized wheelchair, occasional use of crutches and his Dad's arms.

Unforgettably Bryan was released from being an inpatient at the hospital on June 14, 2007. It was my 49th birthday. From this point forward, as an outpatient, Bryan was required to live on base at Walter Reed. He was assigned to the Mologne House and would be required to attend formation every morning. Formation appeared to be the only activity the Marine Corp required of him, and they were insistent that he attend.

Little to no interest was shown in his actual recovery process nor was there a plan for Bryan's rehabilitation. We were invited to continue to stay and help him in his recovery. We couldn't imagine how Bryan would be able to navigate his own recovery with his existing medical challenges and his diminished short term-memory. We agreed to remain.

We stayed in various places on the sprawling grounds of Walter Reed including the Mologne House. The rooms at the Mologne House were reminiscent of a Holiday Inn. There were 2 double beds and a normal bathroom. The lobby of the Mologne House spoke of grander bygone days. The architecture was in the Georgian revival style and it was quite impressive. It had been overtaken by the wounded and their families. Upon entry one could be reduced to tears by the shock of what the eyes beheld. The sober unforgettable memory lingers forever in my mind. Young people missing arms, missing legs, wearing skull caps to protect their own missing skulls, missing eyes, disfigured faces, many in wheelchairs and leaning on crutches waiting in long lines for their turn in the elevator to take them to their floor.

The Mologne House along with the base support systems were overwhelmed. The army base simply was not equipped for the number of casualties and family members that steadily poured through the doors.

The base was like a small town that had been overtaken by displaced people with great needs. The stores where you buy food and clothing were packed and quantity was low. Housing services were in short supply. Transportations services were lacking. Buses and taxis had long waits. Security services were needed. Trash collections overflowed. Parking places were impossible to find. Tempers were short and lines were long. Places to eat were few and shortages were normal. Military personnel that normally staffed these services were deployed to the battlefield, leaving the positions to be filled by civilian contractors.

Turmoil ensued as two different worlds, military and civilian, converged and clashed daily. It was a grueling existence where our lives centered around the basics of life and of course the all-important "formation." Daily it was a search for three meals and waiting to do laundry in the limited facilities complicated by too few washers and dryers that actually worked.

Thankfully we were allowed to travel back to Colorado in June for a 10-day medical leave when in desperation I wished out loud that I could just go home. The attending doctor said sure and my wish was granted by a piece of paper with a doctor's signature.

In Grand Junction Bryan received a hero's welcome at the airport. A limousine took us the 45-minute drive to Delta escorted by the police, the Patriot Guard motorcycle club and various others in the accompanying motor parade. Bryan was met by hundreds of well-wishers that lined main street to complete his welcome home. We were so blessed to be home! We surrounded ourselves with our grandchildren and received many friends and visitors. Bryan's old high school buddies carted him away and only returned him at bedtime.

In the short time we were home we were contacted by an owner of a construction company based in Grand Junction. He came to our home and presented us with a very generous offer to build an addition on to the back of our older home to insure it would be wheelchair accessible when Bryan returned home to stay. He gave us the name of an architect who was willing to donate his expertise to draw up plans for an addition to our house. They would make it handicap accessible for our son. The construction company would then procure donated materials needed from local businesses and build the addition at their expense. We saw it as an answer to a future need and were overcome with thankfulness. The plan was set in process by contacting the architect.

Bryan's healing accelerated while we were home, but all too soon, we were required to be back in Washington, D.C. When we returned, we had been relocated to a nearby hotel as there was no longer room at the Mologne House. Bryan would still be required to be on base at formation each morning. They would move us back to the base when a room became available.

The summer months crawled by with trips to the mall, watching movies and going out to find food. I was frustrated by how infrequent his rehab was. We longed to be home.

I took it upon myself to seek out appointments for our son in the various walk-in clinics that spilled over with waiting wounded military personnel.

Once inside the system I pleaded concerns I had about Bryan's lack of rehab and was referred to additional doctors and appointments. Soon, armed with a plan I had put together for his recovery, we were kept busy going to appointments. I couldn't comprehend how they expected my son to get well if he was left on his own to acquire help. Surely, they didn't expect his presence at formation would help him recover? My goal was to see my son improve to the point we could all go home and continue his extensive recovery in our community.

Forty-five days after he became an outpatient, Bryan's femur was finally healed enough to bear his weight. The long-anticipated process of being fitted for his first leg could begin. We now had the prosthetic clinic visits to add to our schedule.

Bryan celebrated his twenty-first birthday on September 2, with an unexpected extended stay in the hospital with surgery for a painful bowel obstruction. It was a setback that alarmed us all and presented us with a growing desire to wrap up our time at Walter Reed.

Hollie departed in September, shortly after Bryan's birthday to resume her life in Colorado. Fortunately, our separation from Hollie was made easier as Bryan was given another medical release to go home for 10 days to recover from his unexpected surgery.

As expected, the healing days of being home flew by and soon we were required to board a plane in Grand Junction and return to Washington, D.C.

No sooner had Craig, Bryan and I returned to Walter Reed from our brief trip home, when Craig was called to present himself to the office of the Navy-Marine Corps Relief Society. Once there they shamed and pressured him to go back to Colorado in October and resume work.

They had been granting us financial help to pay our household bills but were no longer willing to do so. They felt it was time for Bryan's dad to go home. We greatly appreciated their help in our great time of need, but it was a grave mistake to pressure Craig to leave Bryan and return home.

Craig was not only Bryan's father he was Bryan's mentor, spiritual leader and biggest fan. It had a negative effect on our son almost overnight. Having to say goodbye to Craig was a deeply felt loss suffered by both Bryan and me.

We were further devastated when Sergeant Tobias told us that Bryan would not be allowed to transfer to the VA in Grand Junction after all. His presence would be required in D.C. for an additional year.

Bryan receiving Purple Heart at Mologne House.

Chapter 25
THE FALL

The verdict that denied our request to go home for rehab was like a sentence handed down and Walter Reed became the prison. Bryan's hope was shattered. The decision appeared to activate his TBI (traumatic brain injury) symptoms to an alarming level.

I had worked so hard to insure his transfer to Grand Junction and was physically shocked by their decision. We all knew Bryan would never go back to active military service. His injuries were too severe.

The thought of having to endure another year away from home without reinforcements drained our already depleted hope. Another year?? It was impossible to conceive the despair it provoked in our lives. Bryan and I desperately needed to be home. Life had become harsh and frightening.

As I attempted to get my head around the thought of life at Walter Reed for an additional year, I knew I would need a workable plan. I didn't know where Bryan was in the system and I didn't understand why it made a difference that we stay at Walter Reed. Nothing was happening here that couldn't happen at home, I reasoned. Doctors that he had seen were no longer available. They too had been deployed. I was chasing myself in circles trying to get help.

In the middle of October as I was attempting to get desperately needed help for Bryan's Traumatic Brain Injury (TBI), I was dismayed to finally discover that Bryan was supposed to have had a caseworker the entire time he had been at Walter Reed.

They regretted that Bryan had fell through the cracks and that it had fallen on me to fulfill the role of caseworker.

We had been there June, July, August, September and part of October and they didn't know Bryan existed? They were sorry?? October and November of 2007 were very difficult for Bryan and me as we felt isolated, alone and overwhelmed.

I continued with great effort to help my son keep all his many doctor appointments, physical therapy sessions, formations, and the most hated of all his TBI appointments.

Have you ever tried to get a Marine to do something he doesn't intend to do?

His TBI appointment required me to drive in my car with him as a passenger to the VA in downtown D.C. traffic. This one trip triggered his PTSD every time. It was always a trip to remember.

Bryan's traumatic brain injury severely damaged his frontal lobe. Some of the common effects of injury are sudden changes in behavior including aggression. Another troubling effect is impaired moral judgment which is the ability to discern right from wrong along with the loss of the ability to relate to the emotions of others.

Bryan's TBI was overtaking his compassionate, loving personality, and he was increasingly negative, stubborn, unmotivated and on occasion verbally violent to me and others especially when we were in the car. All TBI's manifest themselves in bewildering and frightful ways and Bryan's was no exception.

It had been hard enough to keep him motivated in the summer months when he was cooperating and I had reinforcements. Now it was only with great difficulty that I was able to get him to physical therapy. With his hope crushed, his cooperation ceased. He was becoming increasingly bitter and would no longer go to church with me. Often times, childishly he would walk on the opposite side of the sidewalk from me when I insisted that he go to PT or a doctor's appointment.

I was emotionally and physically exhausted from the months of continued trauma of Bryan's deteriorating mental health. I had lost 50 pounds and my own health was steadily eroding. We were both lost in a free fall inside a black hole at Walter Reed.

There was no way I could leave him to cope by himself and go home. His diminished memory made that option impossible.

I continued to appeal to the Marine Corps to allow me to take my son home.

In the meantime, Bryan existed in a room by himself. I could no longer withstand his compulsion to stay awake all night, every night, playing loud video games at the foot of my bed. Bryan was simply too afraid to go to sleep at night. He was fearful that the darkness would pull him back into the prison of unconsciousness forever.

For the first time I was alone where I could lament. My grief was so heavy I thought I would be crushed under the weight of sorrow, loneliness and distress. I was in the active process of losing my son, the part of him that made him Bryan. I was overcome. I had a front row seat to the futility of being isolated in D.C. away from family for 10 minutes of formation each day! It was outrageous!

My son needed help and he was not getting it at Walter Reed. He along with the few Marines that were there were like Neverland's lost boys left on their own. Misplaced. Forgotten. It was not acceptable!

Chapter 26
TRANSITIONS

In late November, I was able to persuade the Marine Corps to allow Bryan and me to go back to Colorado for a much-needed break from each other and the downward spiral of life at Walter Reed. This only happened after I was admitted to the hospital for a brief stay as a result of failing health. It was surreal. Bryan was now standing by me in my hospital room and I was the patient.

The doctor notified the Marine Corps that it was critical for me to be allowed to get out of the system and go home. He concluded that I was on the verge of physical exhaustion. It was understood that we would come back before the holidays to receive our final orders to transfer to the VA in Grand Junction.

We continued to reach out on Caringbridge and plead with believers to pray for our son to be allowed to receive treatment in Colorado. By this time there had been over 120,000 visits to his site. We believed God heard each prayer sent forth on the behalf of our son and that the sovereign God would answer in his timing according to His great grace.

Once back in Colorado, I told Bryan that I would go back to Walter Reed with him after the Christmas break if he would promise to attend physical therapy while we were at home. He agreed but did not follow through on his commitment.

It was during the Christmas break that it became apparent that I would no longer be the one to go back with Bryan. I was disheartened by Bryan's refusal to honor his word.

Thinking I had to stand firm to what I had told my son, I did not go back with him after the holidays. It broke my heart and confused Bryan. Even to this date I'm not sure I made the right decision. I had yet to fully grasp the depth of the effects of Bryan's brain injury on his behavior.

Craig returned with Bryan for a few additional weeks to help him get settled back in his room and with his routine of rehab. Craig was there to be with Bryan as he had oral surgery. The bone grafting process for the replacement of his missing teeth had finally begun.

Craig's final goal before coming home was to help our son start his med-boards and transition out of the Marine Corps. and into the VA. We knew a decision must be made in each wounded warrior's case as to whether he would be medically retired or whether he would be required to return to active duty. We were aware that the med-board process was lengthy and involved teams of doctors going over medical records and submitting reports and publishing their findings.

On January 22, 2008, Craig wrote the following entry on the Caringbridge site.

All morning long Bryan had meetings at Bethesda for his med-boards. It was a very good first step and fact-finding trip. We know a lot more of what to expect and maybe a little more about the timing etc. It had seemed like a huge and challenging hurdle for Bryan, but now seems more bite sized and do-able.

The big deal of the day was connecting back up with all of the old crew from 5 east. When Bryan was last wheeled out of there in late April 2007, he did not quite look like he did today. It was such a shock for all of his caregivers from then to see him now. He was basically immobile when he left, had just had his trache out about a week and was a very weak and physically challenged young man. To see him walk back in and standing tall was a sight for all to see. So many miracles occurred during his stay there. So many incredible answers to so many prayers. I do not have enough adjectives to express all that is going through my head about those 2 months.

As the crowning jewel of all our contacts we met today, we stopped and were able to visit briefly with his original attending surgeon, the quarterback, as we affectionately called him. Dr. Liston was speechless as Bryan stood to greet him today. Dr. Liston and his team performed over 28 surgeries on Bryan in his stay there. It was so good to be able to personally thank so many who played such a major role in Bryan's early intensive care. I only wish all of you who have been following this story could meet some of these dear and precious folks. God knows each and every one of them and we believe that He will reward them all for the kindnesses they have shown us over this past year.

After a year like we had in 2007 one might be tempted to ask why? I will leave you with a quote from the apostle Paul who does not have all of the answers, but he is ok with that. "Now we see things imperfectly as in a poor mirror, but then we will see everything with perfect clarity. All that I know now is partial and incomplete, but then I will know everything completely, just as God knows me now."

1 Corinthians 13:12
One day it will be clear.
Craig

Dr. Liston and Bryan

With great effort we finally convinced the Marine Corps that it was in Bryan's and our family's best interest to be allowed to transfer his care to the local VA in Grand Junction, Colorado. Once there Craig would be able to work and be part of Bryan's caregiving. Bryan was accepted into the beginning of a new pilot program for the med-board process. Early projections had him to be done with all the paperwork and appointments and headed back to Colorado in early March. With much rejoicing we saw the hand of God in allowing our son to fly home one year to the precise date of the IED blast, February 28, 2008.

Chapter 27
BACK HOME

In Bryan's absence we had been anticipating making structural changes to our house to make it handicap accessible for our son. We had spent months working with an architect who had donated his expertise to design an addition that was fully wheelchair accessible. Imagine our great disappointment when the local construction company failed to keep their commitment to procure building materials and build the addition. Believing the renovation was needed to make Bryan feel at home, we built it at our own expense. It was not a wise decision. We depleted the entirety of our resources. After the initial excitement of having our son home with us he began to gradually distance himself from us and rarely came home to sleep in his own bed.

Night after night I would lay in bed and listen intently for any sound that might indicate our son was letting himself in. It was emotionally difficult and life-altering to come to terms with, but our son moved out of our home within weeks of coming home having never benefited from the changes we had made to welcome him home.

Over the course of the next ten months we worked diligently to ensure our son kept his appointments, but it became increasingly apparent that he no longer considered himself under our authority. We were dismayed, perplexed and wounded.

The following year was extremely difficult as we attempted to come to terms with all the permanent changes in our lives. Craig was never able to financially recover from time away from his business though he worked relentlessly in pursuit. Our son-in-law Isaiah had worked tirelessly to keep the business going in Craig's absence, but the stock market and housing crash of 2009 eventually made its effect on construction's bottom line. Our way of life that we had known was gone.

We worked relentlessly to help our son through his med boards and Bryan attempted to go to college for a semester but was unable to continue.

Bryan was medically retired from the Marine Corps on Nov 30, 2008. He is 100% disabled.

EPILOGUE

The years following Bryan's medical retirement from the Marine Corps have been some of the most distressing of our lifetime. We suffered as we were witnesses to our son's destructive behavior against his own life. He lived life recklessly as if he indeed was seeking the very death he had been rescued from.

The devastating effects of Bryan's TBI and the frightening changes in our son's personality broke our hearts. His lack of empathy and indifference towards us broke our spirits. We found no help even as we searched along the darkening path.

Mentally, I knew our way of life had changed, but once we got home from D.C. it became a reality that had to be lived out. New wounds were inflicted. A portion of Psalm 103, verse 15 and 16 played out in our lives. *As for man, his days are like grass, he flourishes like a flower of the field; the wind blows over it and it is gone, and its place remembers it no more.*

We had been absent from our home in Delta for months and months and our *place* in our community, our *church*, and in the lives of people we had counted as dear seemed to have evaporated.

As we search for a way to belong, we found that our *place remembered us* no more. Life had gone forward all around us and after the initial welcome home, it was clear we had lost our place, and we felt as invisible as the winds that blew outside our windows.

Gone was the most important place in our lives, our church. Our place of worship, fellowship, and spiritual nourishment had shuttered its doors and its members had dispersed like seed in the wind. No shepherd came looking for us and we were lost.

Nothing had been left unchanged and certainly not us. The winds of time blew bitter cold against the doors of our mortal bodies. Craig was physically and emotionally exhausted when he was thrust back into his business. His spiritual reserves needed replenishing, too. It would have been a balm of healing if he had been given time to recover, but the currents of financial change had blown through our lives and there was no time for rest. Our son-in- law Isaiah, who had stepped in to take over for Craig when disaster stuck, was spent. His wife, our daughter Jennifer, had seen her new business fail as a result of both her husband's inability to be as involved as needed and my lack of presence as her main employee. The grandchildren needed *both* their parents, and Jennifer and Isaiah needed their lives back.

Our daughter Hollie Mae had stepped away from her schooling, her job, and had let her apartment go. Life had changed for her and though she had willingly made these sacrifices there was a price to be paid.

Our son paid the biggest price of all. I had envisioned that Bryan would see with clarity God's miracles as he daily dressed his scarred body. I predicted that he would be quick to embrace Christ and his direction for his life. I believe I had expectations that Christ himself never had. My assumptions were not realistic and strained our relationship. I was naive about the complicated issues of traumatic brain injuries. Bryan had been through devastating brain trauma that deeply affected his personality and his decision-making capabilities. He had difficulty knowing right from wrong. How in the world, Christian, can one fathom what that one dilemma implies? Is Christianity indeed just a list of dos and don'ts? His journey through recovery would be between him and his God in a time frame that *continues* in a personal relationship. He would need to be surrounded by believers who care enough to do more than just thank him for his service *if* he is to grow into the ministry God has for him. Perhaps one day the military will step up and address the needs and special challenges of those who have paid such a steep price for the cause of freedom. Perhaps they will acknowledge the price paid by the immediate family and not just spouses and children. Mothers, fathers, sisters and brothers also suffer immeasurably when their loved one is gravely injured and there is no recovery help discernable. Families pay a price that few in our country understand, including those in our pulpits and church pews.

I was deeply sorrowful. Life looked nothing like we had longed for when we had dreamed of being back home. Lacking the physical hands and feet of the body of Christ like we had had in D.C., we felt abandoned. We were consumed in our flesh and we were shell-shocked by what we had gone through. We were only too aware that we needed help. Physical and spiritual help! We were wounded and we were bleeding-out. It seemed impossible to walk into our future as the past pulled us deeper into the need to understand what had just happened to us.

We became an intellectual problem to be solved for some. Why couldn't we just put our past behind us and get on with life? Why couldn't we realize that our lack of faith was front and center and had compounded our difficulties both in the midst of our time in D.C. and in the aftermath of the storm. Others thought it was as simple as telling us what we needed. You need rest. You need to find help. You need to go to the doctor. You need money to save your home. And you should pay your bills.

It was like telling a thirsty man: "I know what you need! You need water!! Then walking away pleased with yourself for the illusion of helping but never offering a sip of the water you were drinking while you spoke.

Soon I felt fear and condemnation drawing me into a pit of what *ifs*. What if my son was called to give an account for disregarding the life that been restored to him, as some who wagged their fingers at Bryan's behavior suggested? I felt fear's clammy fingers squeezing peace from my mind, drip by drip. Fear of what might happen next. And what became the consuming fear... *what if I lived to see it?*

Life was uncontrollable. Our son was out from under our protection. We feared for his safety. We grieved choices he made. These hard events too numerous to recount continued to roll over us like waves without reprieve. I had expected the storm to end once and for all and yet it continued fiercely. I looked at the waves and wondered what would happen if I just let go.

I was loosening my grip on courage as strength failed and bravery felt unattainable. My own flesh was betraying me with bouts of anxiety, uncontrolled trembling, vicious nightmares and flashbacks of the past. I felt a thick covering of fear pressing into me like a weighted blanket. I was fearful that the relentless storm had altered the landscape of our family relationships forever. We struggled lacking strength to minister to our own. We each returned to our darkened corners separately to wrestle with waves of disappointments. Communication became difficult with each other. Had our own speaking languages been confounded like those in the biblical account of the Tower of Babel?

We attempted to become a part of a new body of believers in our community, but we were in such deep need of spiritual help and healing that we failed to enter in. Craig and I both sunk into major clinical depression brought on by unresolved situational depression. It was a time of numbness except for loneliness and sadness. Our love for one another was not enough to help each other out of the pit, as we suffered in silence unable to give spoken words to our anguished thoughts.

I found it much easier to lay down my weary, spent self and surrender to the comfort of my sofa. I was held prisoner by clammy fear and by flashbacks and nightmares that consumed my days and nights.

I knew the presence of the Holy Spirit was in me, but I was pulled by fear that was so loud I could barely hear the still small voice of the comforter. He pulled up a chair and stayed with me in my quietness and recounted to me His promises that seemed to ring shallow in my despair. The words spoken by my son to me on the stairs all those years ago haunted me. "Mother don't lose your faith. I'm afraid you will lose your faith." Was that what was happening to me? Was I losing my faith? What was happening in me?

The doctor determined I was experiencing what they used to call a good old-fashioned nervous breakdown. My body finally said enough. The psychiatrist who we could only afford to see a handful of times, pronounced that I had undiagnosed PTSD from the events of my childhood that had resurfaced, being freshly traumatized by all that had occurred to our family. The internal wrestling to control my bodily responses was intense. All I knew to do was wait on God to come to my rescue by releasing me from this fearful world. I longed to enter my eternal rest. "It's enough Lord! Take my life!" I pleaded. It was always a surprise to me that I woke up the next day. I never meant too.

In the strange quietness of my withdrawal from life I was diagnosed with breast cancer. Suddenly I was confronted with the prospect that I might gain my desire to leave this world behind.

That spring of 2009, shortly after the diagnosis, Bryan came to visit me. As I listened to him recount the dramatic ironies of our lives, that he should lose a very personal part of his body and now I was to lose a very personal part of mine, he wanted to make a pact with me. He told me he would fight to live if I would fight too. With that heart-to-heart encounter, I had a tiny seed of hope deposited in my heart. It took root. I realized that maybe I *did* indeed want to fight to live. Shortly after that encounter I had a double mastectomy along with a large mass removed from my abdomen. Recovery was spent close to home as I was becoming increasingly uncomfortable in public settings and preferred the quietness of my safe place. I felt decidedly ugly and had a pharmacy in my bedside drawer.

The medical bills piled up, and with the downturn in the economy, we couldn't pay current bills nor the taxes that haunted from back in April of 2007 when we were at Bethesda. We made the distressing decision to move from our much-loved family home in order to sell and recoup finances to pay medical bills so I could continue treatment. The house never sold so we rented it out. The renters refused to pay rent when they became aware that we might lose the house they were living in. The court allowed them to stay there without paying rent till the house foreclosed. We lost our home in 2011.

My husband and I grieved over our lost sense of place along with the disappearance of material possessions gathered over our years of marriage. Our storage units were ransacked, and beloved items carried away. This painful adversity devastated us further as it uncovered intense feelings of failure. Owning a home was a part of the American dream we had long ago bought into. We became homeless. In the end, after we lost our family home, we moved five times to places we had to remodel for the payment of rent to live there.

Life had become much harder but God's unique provisions, His kindnesses of which there were many, were recognized daily. He drew me to repent of my doubts of His goodness. His grace granted desire to live and Truth taught me to trust Him again. It was a labored journey.

I was persuaded by the Spirit to start back to church again when in His still small voice He responded to my whimper for continued understanding. "I just can't go back to church. I just can't! It's too far away anyway, and I don't feel like getting dressed up only to have to make excuses for why I cry all the time!!" It was too far away! We had been going to a church in Grand Junction with Hollie the few times we had attended. And I *did cry* a lot. Craig and I both did. It was not always out of sorrow as some would judge. We were so humbled by all that God had salvaged out of the debris of the never-ending stormy blast. This *one* truth was always front and center in our praise. God has been so *very merciful* to us. We had been allowed to keep our precious son. We had been allowed to be involved in the lives of our equally precious daughters and grandchildren. I had made it past the five-year mark for cancer survivors. Bryan was getting better. God was becoming part of his life again, if ever so slowly. And Craig and I had not given up believing we would be healed too.

Can you walk across the street?

I was startled. There was an Assembly of God church literally steps away from my borrowed front door.

Can you walk across the street? Again, I heard His voice.

I looked down at the old top and stained jeans I had on. We had been doing hard physical labor at the house we lived in. All we did was work. I cried as I walked across the street to renew my commitment to the body of Christ.

I realized the enemy of my soul had been trying to destroy my understanding of who God is by attempting to propagate the doubts I had in my heart. He had argued that God was not to be trusted and wasn't really loving. He shot darts of doubt and confusion when I pondered the tragedies and cruelties in our lives over the past years.

The enemy desired to divert me from focusing on the true character of God by directing my attention to things God did allow to be taken. He wanted me to dwell on the injustices of life and entertain the possibility that God himself could be unjust. I succumbed to his tactics for a season. I was no better than Eve in the garden when she was confronted with a liar and gave him an audience.

The enemy's crowded accusations along with my distorted view of God was shattered. He failed, because the image I now have is of a much greater, ever more HOLY God than my mind can comprehend. I had thought as His child I deserved the suffering to stop at some point. I am not deserving at *any* point. I am not deserving of one good thing. I am totally corrupted in my mind, will, emotions and in my flesh. I deserve only judgement. What God gave me in the gift of salvation is pure grace. After all these events have passed, He is before all else my Father, but He is so much more than just my Father. He is righteous. He is frightful in executing His sovereign decrees. He takes counsel form no one — especially from His daughter.

I rejected the enemy's lies and embraced my faith that had been permanently written on my heart by my Father. Though my faith had faltered for a season it was not dead and had proved to be genuine.

The testing of my faith drew me into deeper study of the Word of God and urged me to consider the moment by moment importance of perseverance for the continuing journey. All storms will end one day.

I was granted fresh strength and committed to educate myself to understand my son's brain injury more fully. I realized that his behavior was not an act of rebellion but a clear result of the trauma he had endured. I loved my son unconditionally despite his behavior, and thus prayed with new insight and faith. I did whatever I could to be a part of his world.

Over the passage of time, God's never-ending grace continues to envelope my son and bring to him healing of mind and spirit. Our merciful Father answered our prayers and gifted him with a loving mate. She has blessed us all.

Our son and his lovely bride were married in beautiful Colorado in 2014. Bryan and his wife, Rhyann, relocated to the place of his birth where they live a mere 10-minute drive from Craig and me in rural Indiana. Our daughter Hollie and her husband Diego have two beautiful toddlers and are at home on the East coast. Jennifer and Isaiah, along with the four *short ones* who are now teenagers, live full lives in Colorado.

Currently Craig and I live in the Midwest where our faithful loving God is always at work in our lives as together, we cry out to him for healing that *continues* 12 years later. One day we believe the storm will end. One day.

I wish I could write a fairy-tale ending that would satisfy. We all love happy-endings. I wish I could testify that we are completely healed from the trauma that has changed us forever. I cannot. There are no easy answers, but God is faithful. Healing takes as long as it takes. God is the author of our story and He will include an ending that will be beyond all we could ever ask or imagine! We are learning to celebrate life again trusting daily in the all sufficient Father. A few months ago, we celebrated our 40th wedding anniversary. We stand amazed.

Bryan and his Marine brothers travel on Memorial Day each year to honor fallen vehicle commander Sgt. Chad M. Allen who paid the ultimate price in the attack that severely injured Bryan.

Bryan standing guard.

Bryan and his lovely wife Rhyann were married in the beautiful mountains of Colorado and now reside in Indiana.

DEDICATION

I will always give thanks to our God for those of you who invested time in prayer and intercession for our precious son. Together we did mighty exploits in the heavenlies as we cried for the life of a young Marine son.

Notes:

[1] Song ID: 39047
  Song Title: Everlasting God Writers: Brenton Brown, Ken Riley Label
  Copy: Copyright © Thankyou Music (PRS) (adm. Worldwide at
  Capitol CMGPublising.com excluding Europe which is adm.
  By Integrity Music, part of David C. Cook family.
  Songs@integritymusic.com) All rights reserved. Used by permission

[2] Song ID: 80288
  Song Title: I Will Lift My Eyes Writers: Bebo Norman, Jason Ingram
  Copyright ©2006 New Spring Publishing INC, Appstreet Music
  CapitolCMGPublising. All rights reserved. Used by permission

[3] Batterson, Mark, In a Pit With a Lion on a Snowy Day,
  Multnoma Penguin Random House LLC, NY 2006

[4] Song ID: 1156881
  Song Title: Praise You in This Storm Writers: John Mark Hall/Bernie
  Herms
  Copyright ©2019 Essential Music Publishing, Be Essential Songs
  Essential Music Publishing.co. All rights reserved. Used by permision.

Made in the USA
Lexington, KY
17 July 2019